Hero Education

A Scholar Phase Guidebook For Teens, Parents and Mentors

Oliver DeMille

WWW.TJED.ORG

AN EDUCATION TO MATCH YOUR MISSION

The Leadership Education Library

Volume 1: *A Thomas Jefferson Education: Teaching a Generation of Leaders for the 21st Century*

Volume 2: *Leadership Education: The Phases of Learning*

Volume 3: *Hero Education: A Scholar Phase Guidebook for Teens, Parents and Mentors*

Volume 4: *Thomas Jefferson Education for Teens*

Volume 5: *The Student Whisperer: Inspiring Genius*

Volume 6: *19 Apps: Leadership Education for College Students*

TJEd.org / OliverDeMille.com

Printed in the United States of America.

Cover and book design by Daniel Ruesch Design | danielruesch.net

ISBN 978-0-9907339-6-6

LCCN 2017912865

*"Assume thy greatness,
for the time draws nigh…"*

−VIRGIL

*"Our current educational system is a typewriter
(would you like a wi-fi-connected laptop instead?)"*

−MICHAEL ELLSBERG,
THE EDUCATION OF MILLIONAIRES

Acknowledgements

A special thanks to the following for their wisdom, ideas, creativity, and recommendations for this book: Ian Cox, Oliver James DeMille, Chris Brady, Dan Ruesch, Sara DeMille, Eliza Robinson, Freeborn DeMille and the many readers, editors, mentors and students who reviewed the manuscript and helped make the book better.

Rachel DeMille and Emma Cox provided numerous improvements during each phase of research, writing, re-writing and editing; their input has been invaluable.

Thanks to the many participants in Mentoring in the Classics and online Leadership Education groups for their thoughtful questions, ideas, and ongoing inspiration.

To Walter, Timothy, Samantha
and the other heroes in their generation.
"When the world needs fixing,
God sends a baby...."

Contents

Note to Readers

This book is written with two audiences in mind: (1) the parents and other mentors who work with youth in Scholar Phase, and (2) the youth who are the actual students doing Scholar Phase.

At times, the book speaks directly to adult parents/mentors. At other times, it switches voice, and speaks directly to the youth. At still other times, it simultaneously addresses both.

It is important for both Scholar Phase youth and their adult mentors to read all of these sections and understand both sides of the Scholar Phase mentoring relationship and process.

What is Hero Education?

The goals of education matter. As C.S. Lewis pointed out in his classic book *The Abolition of Man*, those who structure and manage any educational system can either emphasize great leadership learning or design something more mediocre. Most students and parents—and even teachers—don't really notice which focus their school or curriculum has chosen. But the differences are significant.

Through history, the royal and wealthy classes have tended to emphasize the kind of education that brought their children face to face with greatness, by utilizing the greatest books and leading classics, along with individualized mentoring, thus preparing their youth to eventually take up the mantle of leadership in the various fields of the economy and society. In contrast, many in the lower classes have been left to settle for lesser goals such as mere literacy, or whatever was necessary to get and maintain a job.

In free nations, the middle classes have had a choice concerning the education of their children: on the one hand, standardized conveyor-belt training designed to prepare the young for a steady job and even career promotion, or on the other hand a truly great education to help them join the ranks of leadership in their chosen fields. In short: conveyor-belt education, or hero education.

The same choice is key today. Those who seek the kind of education necessary for tomorrow's leaders won't settle for anything less than genuine leadership education. Every person has genius inside, something unique to that individual that can truly improve the world. Every student is a potential hero, one who achieves great things and serves others in great ways. Those who choose to accept the path of great education naturally develop their leadership and service. That's hero education. In the new globalized and increasingly competitive economy, the need for more people to engage authentic hero education has never been greater.

This book is an urgent call to youth, parents, teachers and leaders to fully embrace Hero Education. It is time for more students to get a truly great leadership education. This book shows you how...

BOOK ONE

FOUNDATION FOR SUCCESS

*"Reading furnishes the mind only
with materials of knowledge; it is thinking
that makes what we read ours."*

–JOHN LOCKE

INTRODUCTION
The 9 Skills

"We have forgotten what it means to be truly educated. Ideally, all students would be effective self-educators rather than dependent on experts. When each learner deeply owns his or her education, the quality and quantity of study and overall education increases. Great teachers and schools encourage and teach their students to be effective self-learners."

–EIGHT WORDS FOR EDUCATION [TJED.ORG]

"'Man's habits change more rapidly than his instincts,' the historian Charles Coulston Gillispie once wrote. That's us. We have all the habits of a new age. The phones. The emails. The ADD clicking of our keyboards. The hand sanitizers. Now we need to develop the instincts....
We need to understand that we're not living at a normal moment....
You can't go back from Google to Britannica.... What will replace the NYSE? What will improve on the post office? What will reshape entertainment...? Our educational order is not yet wired for this new age."

–JOSHUA COOPER RAMO

"The education bubble is about to pop—
are you prepared for the aftermath?"

–MICHAEL ELLSBERG

ARDLY anyone gets a great education anymore. Strangely, it is not even the goal in most public, private or home schools around the world. Instead, literacy, credentials, or college prep now mark the high point of most educational ambitions. In fact, marketable test scores and good grades are frequently (and falsely) equated with quality education. The world has largely forgotten the ideal of a Thomas Jefferson level of education, of really understanding the great ideas, of becoming truly wise through exploring, reasoning, pondering, and internalizing the best that humanity and God have offered. We've strayed from the knowledge that **the main purpose of education is to prepare us to truly serve**, dismissing the admonition, "my people perish for lack of knowledge."[1]

As a result, we too often settle for mediocrity for our children and youth, instead of aiming for and working tirelessly to help them achieve greatness. Every young person deserves a truly great education. In fact, all people— young and old—deserve and need a great education. Moreover, the world desperately needs more men and women with an education designed for greatness, not just career placement. Yet too few schools, educators, or even parents conceive of this ideal, let alone making it a top priority. We have allowed things of lesser value to dominate our institutions of learning—and even many of our homes.

There is a very simple reason for this decline: Hardly anyone does Scholar Phase today. Yet Scholar Phase is the keystone of quality learning, and we can express it as an almost certain declaration: Those who do it, get a great education. Those who don't, always get an inferior education—something less than they could have.

And let's face the elephant in the room. Even among those who do TJEd, some earn a truly excellent Scholar Phase, but too many don't. This is also true of many homeschoolers and those in public and private schools as well—even many of those with high test scores and good grades.

It is time to change this.

What is Scholar Phase?

But what, exactly, is Scholar Phase? Put simply, Scholar Phase entails 5,000 hours or more of reading great books in all important fields from history and math to science and social studies, etc., and discussing them in depth (either verbally, or in written formats).

Reading great books and discussing them changes how people think. It drastically increases their *ability* to think—creatively, analytically, innovatively, deeply. It teaches the reader/discusser to have a mind that

---

1   Hosea 4:6

is nimble, agile, sharp, sensible, decisive, creative. It gives readers the knowledge that facilitates depth, the time to acquire real breadth, and the skills that catalyze ability, bring out talent, enhance experience, and increase effectiveness. Great reading, especially when supplemented with ample discussion of such readings, naturally teaches the 9 Skills that are essential for success in the 21st Century. It changes how we think, and how we learn.

Since the 1950s our schools have offered the same basic kind of education. At one point, it was arguably what most people needed, in terms of preparation for economic security. In addition to teaching young people the Three R's of Reading, Writing, and 'Rithmetic, it also trained them to follow orders, be on time to class (and later to work), and do rote, repetitive tasks for most of the day.[2] These were exactly what was needed by most workers in the industrialized economy, and for those who wanted to go to college.

As a result, such schooling was an effective preparation for the jobs and careers most people experienced. But times have changed. We live in a new economy,[3] where technology is replacing, or gearing up to replace, many of the jobs people used to have—an economy where the competition for income is global, intense, and, to a large extent, unpredictable.

Failing Grades

A new kind of education is required if we want our young people to succeed and thrive in the rough-and-tumble economic environment of the 21st Century. Yet most high schools are still operating the old way—with largely unchanged goals, curriculum, or methods. Even homeschool parents—with the best intentions—often revert to the methods that were in place when they were in school.

The result of this scenario is nothing less than catastrophic for many American families, where workers are finding it harder to make a living, keep a job that really pays the bills, or get ahead. Few families are able

---

2   See Alvin Toffler, *The Third Wave* and *Revolutionary Wealth*.
3   For more on this, do an internet and social media search for Future of Work, Disruption, and the IoT.

education prevents debt

to make ends meet without growing levels of debt, and nearly half of American families can't even come up with $400 for an emergency.[4]

Creating this shift in education would be worth it if it came from a conscious decision to change the focus of our schools and homeschools from [ineffective and outdated] economic preparation and job training to something more important. If our schools truly taught children how to gain increased levels of lasting wisdom, improved relationships, and more genuine happiness, there would certainly be those who would choose to sacrifice the emphasis on career prep. Unfortunately, our schools haven't made any real shift from the industrial age focus on job training. The goals remain the same, while the results fall far short of what is needed.

Of course, the true meaning of success is finding one's genuine life purpose, or mission, and truly fulfilling it. This includes being a person of character, and serving others. These are essential parts of quality education, in addition to preparing for financial and career success.

The current education of most youth is not very likely to provide instruction on how to be wise or at peace, nor is it designed to facilitate their preparedness for personal fulfillment, meaningful relationships, or overall life happiness.

It appears that the education of great souls was sacrificed in order to prepare coming generations to provide for their families, and yet, ironically: for the first time in U.S. history most parents feel that their children will probably experience a *lower* standard of living and reduced lifestyle as compared to their parents.

Here's the reality: while an 18-year-old in 1975 or 1986 could succeed (in a job, technical training, or college) with a decent ability to read, write and calculate, along with the skills of showing up to work on time, taking and following orders well, and doing rote work for long hours day after day, these are no longer enough.

---

4   See Neal Gabler, "My Secret Shame," *The Atlantic,* May 2016, 54.

Most schools still prepare young people this way, but far too many of today's newly graduated workers are finding out that this doesn't translate to good jobs or successful careers anymore. Few schools have changed to meet the needs of today's economy. They are patently teaching to nationalized tests, using a conveyor-belt kind of grade-level and grading system, and training young people for the types of jobs that were plentiful from the 1960s and even on into the 1980s and 1990s. But such jobs are increasingly scarce today.

Instead, to survive and especially to thrive in the new economy, today's 18-year-old needs the following 9 Skills:

1. Knowledge and understanding of history, science, math, leadership, writing, public speaking, social studies, language, use of technology, etc.

2. The ability to think creatively, analytically, and independently.

3. The ability to work effectively in teams or alone.

4. The entrepreneurial spirit of seeing opportunity— even when others see only problems.

5. The habit of effectively taking initiative—to look around, see what is needed or what could be accomplished, and then muster the plans, effort, collaborators, and resources to make it happen.

6. The habit of working incredibly hard and maintaining a passion for both the tasks at hand and the long-term goals these tasks are meant to achieve.

7. The tenacity to keep going even when things are very hard, and when faced with criticism and attack.

8. The ingenuity to face setbacks, problems, difficulties and failures, and find ways to overcome them, adapt, and turn them into opportunities.

9. Mastering the skills of learning new things at the rapid pace of technology and change in the 21st Century economy, unlearning old lessons as they become obsolete (without losing the wisdom

of the past), and knowing how to learn and effectively apply new knowledge and skills as soon as they become useful.

Since this ninth skill is the most important of all those needed to succeed in the 21st Century, the agility and energy to be always learning and always mastering new ideas, knowledge, systems, connections and abilities means that we must all become effective "scholars." This is what Scholar Phase is all about: being the kind of person who knows what is happening, understands why it is happening, and is consistently learning and applying whatever is needed to thrive, succeed, and help others do the same.

In other words, every young person today who wants to achieve his or her life purpose, accomplish a great mission to the world, and thrive in a changing economy, needs to experience an effective Scholar Phase. This doesn't refer to the kind of "scholar" we think of in the old Industrial Age, like a professor on campus or a researcher at the scientific think tank. No offense intended to either of those—it's just that when we say "scholar," it has a whole different meaning. Scholar Phase is a 4-5 year educational experience of learning the lessons of the 9 Skills outlined above.

This kind of Scholar Phase is the key to a great education. Those who master the 9 Skills, get one. Those who don't, don't. And let's be clear: Every youth deserves a great education. Not mediocre. Not simply adequate. Not just enough to graduate or pass the exam. We can do better than such trifling goals. We *must* do better if we want our young people to succeed in the real-world economy. This is more than just a fad or trend in our time; it's an imperative.

Each young person can get a truly superb, top-rate, quality education, one that prepares him/her for lasting success in today's world. Anything less is the wrong approach.

Facing Reality

It is not a slight on teachers to say that our modern schools hardly ever teach things like the 9 Skills anymore. (Even the best teachers find themselves with little room to make a difference in these areas, given the current system.) In fact, they seldom did. If young people in the past learned such lessons, it almost always happened outside of the classroom.

As we already discussed, today's 18-, 19-, or 20-year-old needs to know *how to learn*—to master new things at the rapid pace of technology and change in the 21st Century economy, unlearn old lessons that become obsolete, and know how to learn and effectively apply new knowledge and skills as soon as they become useful. The time to learn these vital lessons is during the high school years.

Moreover, in many ways Scholar Phase is the most important part of education, yet it is frequently ignored by many modern schools, parents, teachers, and youth. The modern high school no longer provides what young people need. The class sizes alone make classroom management a priority over content. The result is too much mediocrity in education, even for the students who get high marks. Great education is seldom found in our current schooling environment. It is time for this to change. Indeed, as a society we desperately need the rising generation to engage Scholar Phase. As we effectively teach the 9 Skills, our future is bright.

1

The Keystone

> *"All across America, our 2ⁿᵈ graders score higher on CQ tests than our high schoolers. Evidently, compliance and conformity come at a price…. Creativity Quotient is 3 times more reliable as an indicator of career success than IQ."*
> –ROY H. WILLIAMS

> *"Parents should be wondering, 'Who are the business mentors for my child?' And right now they're putting them in an environment where they have zero business mentors."*
> –SCOTT BANISTER[5]

At the apex of an arch rests the keystone—a central piece, often enlarged and specially designed for aesthetic appeal. It is this keystone that locks all the rest of the stones in place and allows them to bear weight. In terms of one's lifelong education, there is a keystone that locks all the rest in place: It is Scholar Phase.

To make Scholar Phase a reality for most students, we need to change our views about six major issues in modern education. Shifting all of them is essential.

First, great education is not only about getting a job or training for a career, and it is not about mere literacy—it is about preparing a great soul to live his or her great purpose in life. Every person is born with potential greatness inside, with a certain embryonic genius. Such genius is unique to each individual, and when a young person gets a great education it prepares him to do great things.

---

5   Cited in Michael Ellsberg, 2016, *The Education of Millionaires*, 256.

Mediocre education falls short of this potential.

But what do we mean by greatness?

In the TJEd lexicon, greatness is not defined by charisma, fame, power, celebrity, beauty, prowess or feats that are known by all and storied in history books. Certainly none of these is a disqualifier for greatness; but they are not greatness, per se.

When we speak of greatness, we are referring to the character, competence and commitment to *do what is yours to do*. It is a question of integrity, of compassion, of courage—no matter who notices, no matter who knows. Such greatness may indeed turn the tide of a generation, or it may simply bless one person in private. The measure of greatness is not in the magnitude of the life, but in its quality.

The promise of great education is a very different and better world. Imagine a world where every potential Einstein lives up to his promise. Where every potential Teresa, Nikola, Joan, Thomas, James, Margaret or Marie truly achieves all that he or she is capable of doing. When education is mainly about career success, it seldom produces the kind of greatness that is waiting to be refined in so many of our children and youth. They have truly great potential—but instead of educating them for it, the modern school system routinely trains it out of them. It teaches them to fit in, almost above all else. To say nothing of what it signifies in a higher plane of meaning, this is exactly the wrong lesson in the 21st Century economy.

This is an educational model gone terribly wrong. And the world is much poorer and flatter as a result.

Second, great education is the natural result of students coming face-to-face with greatness. This means that truly excellent learning emphasizes the greatest classics and other great materials in the world—in all fields. When our children and youth learn deeply and directly from the greatest books, writers, scientists, inventors, entrepreneurs, thinkers, statesmen, artists, prophets, composers, sages and leaders of human history—and current times—they have the best chance of getting a truly excellent education.

All people need to be able to dig deep and give their very best. The more competitive things become, the more this is true. And today's economy becomes increasingly competitive each year. Rote memorization, passing the test, or getting the scholarship are no longer enough. Youth with this kind of education will keep falling behind. They won't learn the 9 Vital Skills. Nothing teaches these lessons as effectively as the great classics. Indeed, that's what makes a book a classic—the fact that it teaches us about how others have mastered the kind of skills needed to thrive when the competition is high and the challenges are great.

Classics are works—old or new, written or postulated or painted or composed or hypothesized or sung, etc.—that are worth returning to over and over again because you get more from them each time. Those that are less than this simply don't measure up. Works that qualify for this definition of "classics" inspire great learning and great lives. And make no mistake: in a world of increasingly intense competition, mediocrity is a killer. Only reaching for one's potential greatness gives each young person a fighting chance. Not to mention that reaching for greatness almost always leads to a more fulfilling and really *happy* life, and enables those who achieve it to give more meaningful service and truly improve the world around them.

Third, modern education has fallen into the trap of believing that **schooling** *is the goal. In fact, the real goal is* **great learning**. When the focus is on *schooling*, we make educational decisions and build systems that benefit bureaucracies rather than students. This approach is widespread today, and it is the downfall of modern education and the main reason that so many schools fail to give most students what they really need.

The current trend of educational decline will continue until we address this situation. It can be fixed on a large scale, or parents and teachers can address it directly for their own children and classrooms. Again, we must focus on great student learning, not the bureaucratic agendas, systems and checklists of schools and schooling. Find what helps inspire the student to learn most effectively, and focus on that. This is the blueprint for the kind of education that is needed in today's world.

Fourth, for too long we have relied on a carrot-and-stick approach to education. Our modern conveyor-belt schooling system tries to get each generation of students to pursue quality learning, or at least graduation, using rewards and promises of good grades, scholarships, high-paying jobs and successful careers on the one hand (the carrot), and on the other hand a fear of failure, educational shame, and a lifetime of economic struggle for those who don't succeed in school (the stick).

Both of these strategies fall short. The way of great education is neither the carrot nor the stick, but rather "the love affair with learning." When young people learn to truly love learning, to pursue knowledge, wisdom and skills because learning is a passion, a joy, and deeply rewarding in many other ways, they naturally work for and obtain great education.

When you consider the power of a student approaching his education with a will and a purpose born of a love affair with learning, it goes without saying that any other approach is inferior. The carrot, the stick, and the love affair with learning are the three major methods of seeking quality education, and the latter is by far the most effective. Young people who love learning by the time they are age 6, 8, 11, 15 or 27, and who continue on the path of loving to learn—with intrinsic passion and drive to learn, learn, learn—naturally come to love studying as they mature.

Young people who love to study during their teen years, ages 14, 16, 17, and so on, learn more and gain the skills of applying what they acquire, retain and correlate their learning more effectively than their peers who are dependent on the sticks or carrots offered (or enforced) by parents and teachers. Students who love to learn and eventually love to study nearly always get a great education. They do Scholar Phase. They obtain the 9 Skills and corresponding lessons. And they continue to learn, improve, and adapt to the changing needs of the economy, society, and the world around them.

Those who must be driven by extrinsic rewards or fears seldom get a truly excellent education. Human nature dictates that students will tend to do the minimum to gain the promised rewards or avoid negative consequences, but they rarely find their way out of this extrinsically motivated trap and put in the passion, hours, or personal focus to truly excel. And when these artificial incentives end at graduation, very few continue to put in the time or work to increase their knowledge and skills throughout their lives, beyond the minimum required by their job, boss, or career.

Fifth, it is not the job of teachers or parents to educate young people. The idea that this is their main role is a serious and problematic modern myth with two significant aspects:

1. It is not the primary job of teachers and parents to educate youth — rather, it *is the job of the youth to educate themselves.* Any young person whose education or learning habits are dependent on others will find his or her learning and application inferior to those youth who go all in and earn a great education for themselves.

2. The main role of teachers and parents isn't to educate youth, *it is to inspire them to educate themselves.* When adult educators — by example, and through direct help — focus on effectively inspiring young people to get a truly great education through the teen's *own* efforts and choices, it is amazing how much they can help youth pursue true excellence in learning.

   But when the adults are trying to educate the youth — by force or extrinsic rewards — they end up providing mediocre education for well over half of the students in their care. In fact, the percentage is usually even higher; around seventy percent or more of students don't thrive or excel in most modern schools.

Practically speaking, there is no way the parent or teacher could ever give enough *information* to equal a lifetime of avid scholarship and a true love affair with learning. Especially when you consider how small the percentage of their life students spend being informed by even the most dedicated parent or professional educator.

In contrast, when parents and teachers focus on *inspiration,* the result is powerful. Inspiring students to discover and internalize the information in the world for themselves, and to love doing so, is an important and effective role for teachers, and should be combined with the active role of modeling, facilitating, guiding, and *appropriately* "informing" students. This type of great teaching leads to a lifetime of dedicated learning.

These five realities amount to an overhaul of the modern educational system. To summarize:

- Quality education is about greatness, not
  merely literacy or job training.

- Great education naturally occurs when students come
  face-to-face with greatness — the greatest books, ideas,
  people and materials. Nothing else comes close.

- Great *learning*, not schooling, is the goal, and must be the focus.
  The emphasis must be on student needs and mastering the 9 Skills,
  not the agendas of the educational bureaucracy or administration.

- The carrot and stick approaches to education are inferior to
  helping young people fall in love with learning and pursue their
  own great education. This is the crux of quality education.

- The main role of teachers and parents is to help teach
  and inspire young people to take responsibility for their
  own education — and get a great learning experience
  through their own efforts and hard work.

Put these five elements together, and we have the foundation of an excellent Scholar Phase. *Indeed, the sixth major issue in modern education is that very few people — youth or adult — get a Scholar Phase, yet it is the most important part of quality education.* Without Scholar Phase, great education can't be achieved.

The Right Kind of Education

Years ago, we asked what would be needed to help young people get a truly great, quality, Thomas Jefferson-level education in our modern world. What would help today's youth — in large numbers — get an education like Jefferson, Madison, Abigail Adams, Einstein, Da Vinci, Picasso, and the other luminaries?

We need a generation of leaders, but how can we educate them to fulfill their   potential? The truth is that the Jeffersons, Madisons, Abigails and Einsteins of past generations excelled because they loved learning and loved the hard work of study. They loved to apply what they learned in the real world. They had a passion for knowledge, excellence, and improving the world, and they pursued such passions as youth and later as adults.

Like Lincoln, Churchill, and Aristotle, or the fictional Anne of Green Gables (and other great characters in books such as *The Chosen, Bendigo Shafter, Little Women*, and Plutarch's *Lives*, among others) they voluntarily chose to put great learning at the center of their lives.

In our modern environment, how can young people do the same?

The answer to this generational question came from a surprising place. Put simply, Stephen Covey taught the powerful principle that highly effective people learn to "Begin with the End in Mind." In fact, this was one of his famous 7 Habits.

In education, however, we too often forget this step. We offer a child the education we think is normal, or that the experts recommend, or that our local school counselor tells us is expected. But too often the "end" we have in mind is mere literacy, or impressing the neighbors or in-laws with our child's progress reports, or prepping the child for college entrance or career placement.

While some of these goals have merit and likely have their place among a student's plans and goals, they are subordinate to our aim to truly train up a great soul. This aim will of necessity entail literacy, career success, and so forth, but it is much, much more than these.

Even when a child achieves what today passes for basic literacy and job prep, his or her quality of learning is seldom what we would call truly great. Modern education so often fails to deliver on each child's potential. Indeed, even many of the top ten percent of student achievers who test in the highest percentiles and receive prestigious scholarships and college awards too often note that their education feels shallow, vapid, too rote, missing that essential…*something*.

It is lacking the essence, the *je ne sais quoi* of a truly great education. Too many nominal "successes" in our educational system lament that their education was disappointing, like the letdown Pip exemplifies in Dickens' *Great Expectations,* or what C.S. Lewis called the education of "men without chests." In other words, they can pass the tests, but they know their education is largely shallow and lacking in true quality.

People Are Noticing

William Deresiewicz of Yale summarized the education at our Ivy League schools as the training of "Excellent Sheep." In other words, the *creme de la creme* of our educational system, the "best and the brightest," have stratospheric SAT/ACT scores and prestigious degrees, but many are largely trained to be highly-motivated followers, not leaders. They can be woefully deficient in initiative, creativity, grit, tenacity, and innovative skills. The 9 Skills are missing. Scholar Phase is missing.

Bestselling author Seth Godin noted that too much of modern education is simply "a history of compliance."[6] Fitting in, checking off the boxes, becoming part of the system—this approach is the norm, but it leaves far too many of today's young people unprepared for the real economy.[7]

To get the education of the Madisons, Einsteins, and Abigails of today, young people need to love learning and love *studying*. And they need to pursue learning and studying passionately because they *want* to, not in order to get good grades or win awards but because learning—and applying what one has learned to greatly improving the world—is its own reward. They need the kind of awakening Milo experienced in *The Phantom Tollbooth*, or the boost of original and great thinking Emerson saw missing in our schools and wrote about in *Self-Reliance*.

In order for 15- and 16-year-olds to have such innate and self-motivated love of study, we need 13-year-olds who deeply love learning. Yet our schooling system only produces a few such young people. Rather, we turn out approximately 10 percent of students who are passionate about the rewards of academics and top careers (the carrots), and around 20 percent who couldn't care less. Another seventy percent in the middle tend toward mediocre learning and middling job options.

By any measure, such numbers represent a failing grade. Even if the 10 percent were quadrupled, we'd still be failing. Our schools—despite some excellent exceptions—are simply not doing their job. Indeed, our societal

---

6   Cited in Michael Ellsberg, 2012, *The Education of Millionaires,* paperback edition, 251.

7   See *Most Likely to Succeed* by Tony Wagner and Ted Dintersmith, *The Education of Millionaires* by Michael Ellsberg, *The Coming Jobs War* by Jim Clifton, and *Smart People Should Build Things* by Andrew Yang.

experiment with the modern high school is a bust for most students. Without the 9 Skills, our schools simply aren't preparing young people for the real world.

This includes many private, charter and home schools: it's not limited to public institutions. It also includes colleges and universities as well as high schools and the lower grades. While our current school system is good for a few—mainly those pursuing careers in fields like health care and engineering—it lets down too many students. The failures of our educational system are a national disappointment, and a societal tragedy. The system is turning into an economic disaster as well, and this trend seems likely to continue. Much of our modern schooling system is still in decline.

The solution is Scholar Phase.

Prior to the Teenage Years

But to get there, we need to do better in the two earlier phases. Core Phase (generally established in children during the ages 0-8) emphasizes teaching the vital lessons of right and wrong, good and bad, true and false. While these may seem simple, they are incredibly important. Too often our modern Kindergarten thru 4th Grade classes emphasize reading and numerical literacy, when the real focus should also be on the skills of recognizing and promoting what Plato called the good, the true and the beautiful. Such a foundation gives meaning and purpose to reading, writing, and arithmetic—as well as more advanced topics and skills.

When we teach skills and knowledge without infusing them with deep purpose and real meaning, schooling becomes rote for most students, and education becomes a mere exercise in obedience, promptness, and memorization.[8] No wonder well over half of students fail to thrive in such a system.

Great education is so much more. And great education is the natural consequence of learning for a deep purpose. Parents and teachers who use the early years, ages 0-8, to help children catch a vision of such purpose

---

8   See the educational writings of Alvin Toffler, including *PowerShift*, *The Third Wave*, *FutureShock*, and *Revolutionary Wealth*.

(along with standard learning skills) are setting the stage for great education ahead. Those who don't, naturally relegate a majority of students to a future of mediocre or poor education—and misaligned education even for many who do well on tests and achieve high grades.

The most important roles of adults in helping Core Phase students are (1) to read aloud to them (particularly stories that emphasize the vital lessons of right, good, and true), (2) introducing children to great books, art, science and other materials that teach these lessons, and (3) modeling the importance of reading and learning from such materials by personal example. This is the crux of excellent child-centered educational philosophies promoted by the likes of Montessori, Peter Gray, Ken Robinson, and Thomas Jefferson Education's Core Phase.[9]

Once a student has gained a solid Core Phase, Love of Learning Phase (for girls roughly ages 9-12 and boys roughly ages 10-13) focuses on helping older kids and early teens expand their skills, knowledge, and learning—with an emphasis on pursuing areas of personal interest, excitement and passion. Ideally parents and teachers continue to read aloud to young people during this phase, using age-appropriate materials, and engaging more and more verbal discussion of what is being read.

Library trips increase during Love of Learning Phase, students read more, and rabbit trails abound in writing, math, science, art, history and other areas of learning. The emphasis is less on expert-prepared curriculum and more on student projects and experimentation with numerous topics, ideas, authors, and fields of learning. All of this is best pursued under the caring guidance of committed parents and/or mentors and teachers, and with lots of interpersonal discussion about what the student is reading, experiencing, and learning.

The goal is to help the student learn as much as possible, especially in areas of personal interest and passion—and to connect and relate such areas to all the other fields of knowledge. The focus is ideally always on love of learning. This is the Phase of learning so wisely encouraged by great educational thinkers such as Charlotte Mason, John Taylor Gatto,

---

9   More details on Core Phase and Love of Learning Phase are found in *The Phases of Learning* by Oliver and Rachel DeMille, available on Amazon.com or at TJEd.org. Also find more details at TJEd.org.

Andrew Pudewa, Tiffany Earl, Connor Boyack (*Passion-Driven Education*), Sarah MacKenzie (*Teaching from Rest*), Jamie Martin (*Give Your Child the World*), and others.

Young people who experience a full and exciting Love of Learning Phase naturally fall deeply in love not only with learning but also with quality, focused study, thinking, and voluntarily/passionately pushing themselves academically. With the help of committed mentors, somewhere between ages 12 and 14 such students typically become ready for a truly great Scholar Phase.

When this happens, they are on the path of great education. And they learn to settle for nothing less than a great education.

A Change is Necessary

We must change the current approach to high school-level learning. This is a serious issue for a nation that is losing its leadership edge in the world—precisely because we don't effectively teach innovative thinking in most of our schools. The school system routinely teaches students "what to think," not "how to think." This attempts to give them literacy and basic levels of training (such as obedience, fitting into hierarchies, following instructions, and being on time), but doesn't even try to give them world-class *wisdom*, *entrepreneurial* or *thinking skills*.

Scholar Phase does the opposite. Specifically, it drastically improves at least four additional types of learning and thinking skills, as outlined by Roy H. Williams:

> *Fluency.* This measures, according to Williams, "The total number of interpretable, meaningful, and relevant ideas developed in response to the stimulus [the thing the student is reading or thinking about]." This applies to any stimulus or input. Students learn to immediately understand what is needed in any situation and respond, to proactively initiate, formulate goals, and move toward desired outcomes.
>
> *Flexibility.* Students become adept at quickly identifying possible options, noting the differences between them, and determining the

best course of action given the situation, relationships, resources, people involved, and opportunities.

Originality. Learners become skilled at comparing current methods, past successes, and possible new ways of doing things—and mixing these to achieve what they really want. Also, they become adept at getting others to buy in and make the right things happen. They learn from the past, and also creatively innovate as needed.

Elaboration. Students learn to see connections, forecast probable outcomes, and bring together needed pieces or people. They learn to notice details in at least three directions: more specific, more global, and interrelated with other things.

These skills are vital to success, and they are the natural results of Scholar Phase. Students who engage Scholar Phase significantly increase these skills, while the large majority of their peers get weaker in these vital learning categories as they progress through their teen years (at least in the current educational system).

The skills outlined here are a profound, and effective, way of measuring how much a student has actually learned—and to what extent he or she is able to apply valuable knowledge in the real world. As Williams notes, Creativity Quotient is a much more effective gauge of useful learning than IQ (Intelligence Quotient) or even the more recent EQ (Emotional Intelligence).

Moving on From the 1960s

Put simply, our nation needs the rising generation to excel in learning *how* to think. This includes the skills of creativity, ingenuity, initiative, and quality analysis. The new high-tech, globalized market demands these skills—without them, students won't find success in the new realities of the 21st Century economy.

These skills, along with traits like grit, innovativeness, truly independent thinking, effective risk-taking, originality, financial wisdom,[10] the 9 Skills we've already discussed, and tenacity, are the skills of success in the 21st century economy. Yet most schools—from Kindergarten to graduate

---

10   See Chris Brady, 2014, *Financial Fitness for Teens.*

studies—are still operating on the conveyor-belt educational model of the 1950s and 1960s. The skills listed here are largely ignored.

As a result, Americans are struggling to compete in the emerging world economy. The most recent educational trends, at least in the public school system, are built around the concept of "accountability," but this has followed the pattern of A Nation at Risk, Education 2000, No Child Left Behind, Common Core, and reliance on nationalized multiple-choice tests such as the SAT and ACT—meaning that our American education system still emphasizes 1960s-style conformity, rote learning, and institutional compliance rather than quality learning.

Students are sorted into "successful," "mediocre," and "failing" based on criteria that have little to do with real success in the real economy—like how exactly they follow instructions from their superiors, how well they accomplish rote memory exercises, and how well they do repetitive work. While these things were designed to train schoolchildren for success in Industrial Age factories and high-rise office buildings, the new economy no longer rewards such habits or training.

The result is more mediocrity in our schools, a generation of graduates who are less competitive in the global market, a declining share of the world's innovations, and an economy that is headed in the wrong direction. It leads to fewer entrepreneurs and fewer jobs. These trends will continue unless something significant turns things around.

In contrast, Scholar Phase naturally, quickly, and effectively teaches the essential skills outlined herein. Students in Scholar Phase consistently increase their fluency, flexibility, originality and elaboration skills. They quickly gain skills in creativity, analytical thinking, connected thinking, innovation, ingenuity, application of knowledge to real life, etc.

Learning Over Schooling

I suppose it shouldn't surprise anyone that schools and homes focused on innovation and ingenuity are usually promoted by entrepreneurs and innovators rather than by the educational establishment. Parents, teachers and educators who are genuinely interested in great education—more than trying to impress the declining educational bureaucracy—will find that Scholar Phase is an invaluable tool.

It is, in fact, the *indispensible* part of any great education. Find a person with great education, and he or she experienced a Scholar Phase. Give a person a Scholar Phase, and she'll earn a truly great education.

Bestselling author Alvin Toffler wrote in *Revolutionary Wealth* that truly successful parents and schools in the decades ahead will replace rote memorization and a culture of academic conformity with the opposite: creative thinking, personalized learning for each student, and individual mentoring. Another way to say this is simply that great education is based on the principle of helping young people get a truly great Scholar Phase.

Go Great

Beyond economic concerns, Scholar Phase is also the keystone of getting a great education for its own sake. Knowing, understanding, and gaining the wisdom and skills of a great education are all deeply connected with Scholar Phase. Those who get it are educated. Those who don't, aren't.

The great books and great ideas are central to great education. They have so much to teach us, so many lessons that are too often missing in the modern textbook approach to education. For example, consider the following:

> "It is a truth universally acknowledged…"
> –JANE AUSTEN
> *(There are universal truths.)*

> "Are you good men and true?"
> –SHAKESPEARE
> *(Character is key to education, happiness, and life.)*

> "I have spoken. You have heard; you know the facts; now give your decision."
> –ARISTOTLE
> *(Informed decisions are usually better than the uninformed.)*
> *(Choice is the great power of human life.)*

"I do not understand. I pause; I examine."
–MONTAIGNE
(Think before you act.)

"And now abideth faith, hope, charity, these three: but the greatest
of these is charity."
–I CORINTHIANS 13:13
(Great success is based on great love, great sacrifice, and great service.)

"Histories make men wise; poets, witty; the mathematics, subtle;
natural philosophy, deep; moral, grave; logic and rhetoric, able to
contend." [sic]
–FRANCIS BACON
(Get a great education!)

"Not snow, no, nor rain, nor heat, nor night keeps them from
accomplishing their appointed courses with all speed."
–HERODOTUS
(Some things are worth doing no matter what!)

"Up! up! my friend, and clear your looks;
Why all this toil and trouble?"
–WILLIAM WORDSWORTH
(Attitude matters!)
(We choose our attitude.)

"I am Sir Oracle,
And when I ope my lips let no dog bark!" [sic]
–SHAKESPEARE
(Listen to the right voices; and: Don't listen to the wrong voices.)

"Everybody's friend is nobody's."
–SCHOPENHAUER
(Stand for something!)
*(Stand for the right thing, regardless of what
other people might think or say.)*

"All is in flux. Nothing stands still."

−HERACLITUS

*(Become expert on dealing well with change
and turning it into opportunity.)*

"We have heard the pride of Moab...his loftiness, and his
arrogancy, and his pride, and the haughtiness of his heart."

−JEREMIAH 48:29

(Remain always humble!)

"That when the sea was calm, all boats alike
Show'd mastership in floating..."

−SHAKESPEARE

(Become expert on taking wise risks.)

"...laws of nature and nature's God ... endowed by their
Creator..."

−THOMAS JEFFERSON

*(There is a power higher than mankind, and laws outlined by our
Creator that all people must follow if they want to be happy.)*

"Come, go we then togither." [sic]

−SHAKESPEARE"

(Your team—and who is part of it—makes all the difference in life!)

Such lessons—along with important academic knowledge—simply must
be part of learning. If not, the educational model is shallow and flawed. In
Scholar Phase, great education is both the goal and the norm.

The purpose of this book is to show readers how to get a truly great Scholar
Phase—for yourself, your youth (if you are a parent or grandparent), and
your students (if you are a parent or professional educator). The future of
our nation is inextricably connected to the future of Scholar Phase. So is
each child's future success and happiness. In the new economy, Scholar
Phase is simply essential.

---

11   Most of the quotes in this section, and others like them, are found in Arthur Quinn,
     1982, *Figures of Speech: 60 Ways to Turn a Phrase.*

The good news is that you have a great deal of power in this matter. Learn how to deliver a great Scholar Phase, and do so for your children and youth. This will drastically improve their future.

2

The Discussion Method

"From time to time, (the) tribe (gathered) in a circle. They just talked and talked and talked, apparently to no purpose. They made no decisions. There was no leader. And everybody could participate. There may have been wise men or wise women who were listened to a bit more — the older ones — but everybody could talk. The meeting went on, until it finally seemed to stop for no reason at all and the group dispersed. Yet after that, everybody seemed to know what to do, because they understood each other so well. Then they could get together in smaller groups and do something or decide things."

–DAVID BOHM

"'…what is the use of a book,' thought Alice, 'without…conversations?'"

–ALICE IN WONDERLAND

"The value of the teacher isn't sitting there grading [or lecturing]….the value of the teacher is the time she's sitting with students, be it through technology or face-to-face, really providing small-group discussion, providing greater content…. [T]o think more deeply about…students…frees the teacher to spend more time…with her students…. This is the enhanced teacher."

–MALCOLM FRANK, PAUL ROEHRIG, BEN PRING

THERE is another major change we must make in the way we view schooling if we want to provide the kind of education young people need in the 21st Century. Put simply, we must replace the current Lecture Method of, well, *lecturing* with the Discussion Method of learning. In fact, it is almost impossible to overstate the importance of frequent and quality discussion in getting a great education. In most North American educational circles (deeply steeped in the Lecture Method of teaching), the power of "discussion-based learning" is often overlooked and undervalued. And even where it is attempted, the moderators often feel inadequate because they were not raised up in this method of learning, and they are not skilled in facilitating this learning environment.

It is essential to fix this problem before we can truly pursue great education. It's not the books you read, the assignments you complete, or the tests you pass that provide the most important elements of quality education. It's what you actually *learn* from the books and/or assignments.

And, to be clear, what you learn comes partially from reading or doing, but it is drastically influenced by conversations you have about the book, characters, plotlines, ideas, principles, details, difficulties, and other lessons. Who you communicate with about the book or assignment (verbally, in writing, and from cultural sources) is more important than whether or not you read the very best texts or work through the most well-designed curriculum.

Indeed, a combination of reading the greatest books and talking about them with thinking people is the key to truly excellent education. The effective discussion is the quintessential and indispensable element of great learning. But, again, in our modern American educational system few people understand "the discussion" approach.

It is time to remedy this lack. Discussion learning is incredibly effective. For example, consider Victor Hugo's classic *Les Miserables*. It is a masterpiece of great writing, and a formidable work of literature, linguistics, cultural analysis, class/caste commentary, history, moral ethics, and even psychology. It deals with some of the most important human challenges, issues, and struggles, and does so in a powerful way.

Yet Hugo's writing is even more profound because of the way his book inspired additional conversations and creations—from the musical *Les Miserables*, with its inspiring melodies, lyrics and dialogues, to the many movies attempting to capture and convey its most important messages. These follow-up "discussions" to the original book have made it many times more meaningful, powerful, and moving.

Read Like a Billionaire

Such "discussions" can take a number of forms. For example, years ago I read an article that mentioned how certain self-made billionaires consider reading classics vitally important—not assigned reading like we often experience in school, but the act of voluntarily reading for the sake of personal enrichment, pondering and thinking about a great classic or other great book.

With a little research, I learned that many billionaires have a favorite classic that they recommend reading and re-reading. (Indeed, when someone suggests re-reading a certain book, you know it's a great work for him, one that provides recurring life mentoring over time.) Just getting a suggested book to read from a very successful person is a form of "discussing" a book, because it tells you he or she found something important in it—and you can go to the book yourself and look for whatever it has to teach.

For example, the following billionaires recommended these great books:[12]

Steve Jobs: *William Blake's writings*

Like Emerson's essays, the works of William Blake make an artful case for individualism, and the idea that the dreamers, rebels, and those who see how the world could—and should—be different need to make their influence felt. Artists call this viewpoint (of truly being yourself, authentic, not trying to fit in) by the term "romanticism," and it is a powerful perspective.

The influence of Blake's ideas on Jobs and his life are obvious. The more deeply one studies Blake's writings, along with Jobs' biography, the more parallels surface. The connections are fascinating. The question arises: Do you have a great classic that is a life mentor for you like the works of Blake were to Steve Jobs?

Bill Gates: *The Catcher in the Rye*

The message of this classic couldn't be more pointed. Sometimes the key to world progress is for one person to take a stand against the crowd. To sway the course of things. To almost single-handedly turn the tide of human events. One person can make a huge difference.

---

12   "C.E.O. Libraries Reveal Keys to Success," Harriet Rubin, July 21, 2007.

Mark Zuckerberg: Virgil's *Aeneid*

This classic book seems particularly appropriate as a favorite for the founder of Facebook. Virgil's major theme is that the world of his time was in a period of significant change between the old era and the new—and his message of warning was that Rome's leaders needed to embrace the best of the old and the new, and simultaneously reject the worst elements of both.

Virgil wrote of an epic time where the right kind of leadership could nudge the world in the right direction—while the wrong leaders could do the opposite. The connections not only make sense, but they are also instructive to all living in our time. Each child today, and every youth, has the potential to influence the world in striking, even epic, ways.

Richard Branson: *Wild Swans*

This history of three generations of a Chinese family is one of the best books I've ever read. I can see why Branson likes it. It shows how the changing of laws and traditions in a society drastically shift a family's values and adds to their struggles, like an Asian *Fiddler on the Roof*.

It also teaches that certain values remain through many generations, like family relationships and trying to make life economically better for the next generations. *Wild Swans* is a truly great book. In fact, in a world where China is becoming increasingly important to the rest of us, this book should be on most people's classic reading list.

Elon Musk: Asimov's *Foundation* series

This classic sci-fi series causes the reader to see things well beyond the present. In fact, for me this series was one of the most important teachers of how to recognize societal trends and forecast them for not just decades but for centuries ahead. This skill was highly valued in historical French education (for example, in *Democracy in America,* Alexis de Tocqueville accurately predicted the U.S. Civil War decades before it came, and the Cold War between the U.S. and Russia over a century before it arrived; both Montesquieu and Rousseau were effective forecasters as well). Such skills of long-term thinking are also very important in many Asian educational models.

But the same skill is not often a significant part of British-American education. Fortunately, the *Foundation* series teaches readers to think in big, long-term ways that most Europeans and Americans seldom attempt. Musk clearly followed this longer-term approach in his career — taking on such grand projects as developing totally new energy sources, drastically different transportation for the world, and colonizing Mars, for example.

Dee Hock: the *Rubaiyat*

Hock is the father of the credit card and founder of Visa, and he made a lifetime study of a favorite great book, the *Rubaiyat*. While this classic is little known in some circles, its English translation is actually the most popular long-form poem in the English language. It is written in poetic stanzas with four-line hidden codes, which seems appropriate for a favorite book of the founder of the credit card era — who set the stage for a world run by algorithms. Quatrain-based poetry and financial algorithms somehow seem naturally connected.

But beyond this, the content of the poem is powerful and moving. It deals with the purpose of life — what our time here on earth is really about. The book questions whether the real purpose of our lives is money, success, love, family, or something else. Then it discounts each of these, and outlines what its author, Omar Hayyam, believed life is really about — like a shorter and more poetic version of Tolstoy's *War and Peace*.

It is a truly great read, one deeply worthy of a lifetime of study. For anyone who wants to be happy, the *Rubaiyat* is worth re-reading and pondering over and over.

Just knowing that Dee Hock spent many hours in his life studying and deeply thinking about the *Rubaiyat* made me want to read it. Over the years, it has become one of my favorite books. It has taught me so much about what it really means to be happy, and what success in life actually entails. I am so glad Dee Hock "discussed" this truly important book with me. While I've never met him personally, I feel so blessed that his words about this great book introduced me to it and inspired me to take it seriously.

These billionaire-recommended classics—and so many others like them—illustrate the power of the Discussion Method of learning. It's not just about reading a book—it's about who suggests it, why they recommend it, and what you and others say about the book and all it contains. All of these things are part of the "discussion." Mortimer Adler, founder and editor of the Great Books series, called this ongoing discussion of the greatest ideas and principles by an interesting name: "The Great Conversation."

To get a great education, it is important to join this great conversation/discussion. It has been going on for millennia, and it is still progressing today. The only question is whether you will be part of it. And it starts with Scholar Phase.

Read and Discuss

Of course, the discussion of books can also be simple, literal, and direct. Whenever you read something you consider great, moving, or powerful, find a way to discuss it with someone. If nothing else, write about it online—and reply to the responses. Or make a meme or YouTube video to share the most important lessons you learned from the book. This adds to the Great Conversation.

If possible, set up a book club with family members or friends—read a book a month, or more, and meet to discuss what all the participants learned from each book. Just listening to what other people have to say about a book you've recently finished reading will drastically increase how much and how well you learn from it. Not only will you gain new insights into the reading and the tangential rabbit trails that inevitably ensue in discussion with your companions, but you will gain special insights into yourself as you interact with others on this level. You will learn more about the limitations of your assumptions; the uniqueness of your perspective; your strengths and gifts, your deficits and blind spots. Taking part in discussions boosts reading and learning to a whole new level.

Scholar Phase consists of at least 5,000 hours of reading great books and *discussing* them with other people. It is vital to understand that the discussion is just as important as the reading. Indeed, reading without discussing isn't a Scholar Phase. Both are essential.

Simply put: One of the most effective ways to get a truly great education is to read the greatest books in all fields of knowledge, and discuss what you've learned with other people—including peers, parents and teachers, and, when possible, experts who have deep experience in the topics you are reading about. This combination is where the idea of high schools, colleges, and universities originated. And even though too few schools still use this original learning format, it is actually one of the best ways, one of the most ancient, tried-and-true ways, to get a truly superb education. It is the best way to learn the 9 Skills, and to get a true Scholar Phase.

Specifically, there are three essential personas to discuss a book with:

1. You
2. Peers
3. Mentors

Let's address each, one at a time.

Discussions with You

At first blush, it might sound strange to discuss a book with yourself, but this is actually one of the most important types of discussion. Put simply, each time you read, take notes. Write notes in the margins, in a separate notebook, or on your computer or smartphone.

Take notes of things you want to learn, remember, or study more deeply. Moreover, ask questions in writing. For example, if you are reading a great book (say, something by Aristotle) or story (such as Shakespeare's *Romeo and Juliet*), and you aren't sure what a word or phrase means, circle it with your pen and draw a question mark in the margin. (Of course, don't do this with a library book or one you've borrowed from someone else—at least not without the owner's permission.)

By taking notes as you read, you begin a discussion with yourself about the things you are learning from the book. Years ago a mentor suggested that I write the main new lesson I learned on each page in the top margin of that page in every book I read. Today I can go back to books where I used this approach, pull them off the shelf, and skim through them—reading my notes at the top of each page, page after page. I quickly remember what I considered the most important things on each and every page.

In fact, I was in college when I learned this, and I found that it greatly helped me when it came time for final exams. I pulled out the books for my classes and read my notes at the top of each page. It was great for my recall, and I can still go to such books and quickly review them today.

Over the years, as I re-read books more than once, I decided to use a different color of pen the second or third time I read each one. I can tell which notes at the top of each page, and in the margins, came from the first time I read it, or during a later read. Some of my books have numerous colors and very, very full margins. I later began adding sticky notes to pages so I could write more notes even though the margins were completely full.

Now, when I want to read such a book, I find that my notes from years and decades past provide some of the best discussions about the book that I could ever have. Sometimes I disagree with things I wrote many years ago—over time, I've changed my mind or experienced life in ways that make me re-evaluate my more youthful words in the margins. Such discussions with myself are invaluable.

Increased Value

This also adds to the learning value of such books. They have the author's words, of course, but they also contain my own notes—over the course of many readings—that make such volumes literally priceless to me. For example, one of my favorite experiences was getting copies of pages from a book originally owned by John Adams and reading his personal handwritten notes in the margins. This "discussion" with him was even more valuable to me than the words of the actual author.

I have since added my own notes to these copies, so when I read them now I have a four-way dialogue—the author of the book, the notes written by John Adams, my own past notes, and my current thoughts and ideas. Likewise, my daughter borrowed one of my marked-up books for a class she was taking and added her notes to mine in the margins (with my permission), making the book even better. It is now an excellent source of great ideas, questions, debates, and thinking. Indeed, we own books that sport a margin-conversation with sons, daughters, uncles, cousins, etc. What a treasure these are—on so many levels!

Remember, the purpose of great education is learning how to greatly *think*—and how to *apply* great thinking to improve the world. This bears repeating. Great education isn't about learning *what* to think, but rather *how* to think. And, more importantly, how to think and act greatly.

This occurs more effectively when you carry on a conversation with the author—and write down your side of the discussion in notes. Then update and expand your notes as you re-read the book over the years. Such discussions make you a better reader, a better thinker, and often a better leader.

For example, after you have read the first two chapters of a book and added your notes to the margins, and then gone to bed for the night, your book is perfectly poised for you to learn the most from it tomorrow. Why? Because when you pick it up to keep reading, starting in chapter 3, you can first go back and review the notes you wrote yesterday in earlier chapters.

This kind of "discussion" and review greatly improves how much you learn, and upgrades the quality of your learning and thinking. It is part of great education, while mediocre learners skip such note-taking, reviewing, and on-going "discussions" with themselves and the authors they read.

A Big Upgrade

Just this one small change of beginning to read this way from now on will upgrade the quality of your learning and thinking to a whole new level. Once you get used to it, there is no going back. When you read this way (debating with the author in the margins, taking notes, re-reading your notes, and using ?, !, highlighting, underlining, circling, stars, asterisks, lines down the border of a paragraph, etc. to really get the ideas of the book into your mind as you read), you aren't just reading a book—you're truly *learning* a book. And you're deeply *thinking* as you learn. This is great education. This is how to do Scholar Phase.

The first level of discussing a great book is to greatly "discuss" it with yourself. Learn to read books this way, and your education (and the fun of reading and learning) will drastically improve.

Discussions with Peers

Now, to the second level: Imagine that you have finished reading a great classic, such as Shakespeare's *Henry V*, and you are now attending a discussion where four of your best friends, your parents, and their parents have all read the same book and you discuss it together for an hour or more. You start with food or refreshments to make the event even more enjoyable, and you quickly open the book and begin sharing what you learned.

Imagine your dismay as you quickly realize that you have far too many notes in the margins to ever share them all with the whole group. But you skim through your book and see a section that you circled boldly three times, signaling that it was one of the most important things you learned. You raise your hand and share your ideas, based on your notes.

The other participants listen, and some of them nod in agreement with your thoughts. After you finish making your point, one of them agrees with what you said, and shows how she came to the same conclusion — but for an entirely different reason. You are amazed at her insight, and you quickly write a few key words in the margin of your book so you'll remember her comments.

Another participant disagrees with your point, and the whole group discusses the opposing views for a while. Eventually you realize that both perspectives have merit, and both have taught you something important. For example: Henry truly is a great king, no doubt about it. He cares deeply about his men, his kingdom, and its people. He genuinely does have the best interests of both England and France in mind. That was your original point.

But you also realize that your friend's disagreement with you has some merit. Even though Henry is a good king, the system of monarchy and the violence needed to maintain it has some serious flaws. Henry's words about fighting old men and young children are just plain wrong. Your friend is right. No matter how much you like Henry personally, you realize that you're not a fan of monarchy — at least as portrayed in this play. There must be a better way.

As you are thinking about this, and while the participants continue to discuss it from many angles, you glance at a friend's copy of the book, and you notice that his margins are full of handwritten notes like yours. Maybe even more full. You smile, and quickly give up any illusion that you'll be able to share everything you wrote in your margins. You sit back and relax, and enjoy the discussion.

Note that the same kind of discussion can take place in online discussion groups, often with even better results because you can spend more time discussing and also include people across the globe.

Exponential Learning

As you listen to the things people share, you are amazed at some of the ideas that never even crossed your mind as you read the play. You find yourself shaking your head in disagreement at some of the ways people interpret the play. And you realize that you are taking even more notes in the margins as you listen to the discussions than you did when you read the book on your own at home.

When the discussion is over, you laugh, help calendar the next discussion event, and you realize that you are surprised by how much more you learned from the discussion than the reading. You shake your head as you realize you're thinking, *I wish the discussion had lasted twice as long.*

In fact, you suggest that the group meet again to discuss *Henry V* even more deeply, but most of the people disagree and you quickly realize that the majority of participants really want to move on and discuss *Sense and Sensibility* next time. You smile and choose to accept the plans of the group. But you and your friend Jennifer agree to share your additional thoughts and notes, and to debate them with each other online. Then Garth asks to join you.

On the ride home, your dad asks what notes you had written but didn't get to share. You open your book, and spend the next twenty minutes reading, discussing, agreeing and disagreeing, and talking about the words, ideas, characters, and lessons. Your mom joins in, and once you arrive home the three of you sit in the driveway together conversing, discussing the book, and laughing into the night.

Note that in the situation just outlined, the fictional You participated in all three kinds of discussion: with your own notes, with your peers, and with more advanced mentors (the parents). But also note that of the three, your own notes are arguably the most important. In fact, when your friends or the adults in the discussion said something really good, or surprising, or fascinating, you almost always made sure to write these things down in your margin notes. You want to remember them and think about them more deeply.

The truth is that the words of the authors, your peers, and your parents, teachers, mentors and coaches are very valuable for your learning—mainly because they get you thinking, debating, considering, disagreeing, or otherwise making yourself think even more rigorously. And when you are thinking, the ideas you come up with in your own mind are among the most valuable things you learn. Consider how important it is to capture those thoughts—from all three discussions—in the blank spaces of your book!

Another way to carry on the Great Conversation on all three levels is to pass along a single copy of a book, and have several individuals write their notes in it as they read. Books such as this are highly prized in our family, and basically have heirloom status, no matter the value of the original, unannotated work. The level of discourse that takes place in the space between a pen and a paper is nothing short of transformational, and this grows exponentially with each successive reading, and for each reader.

A Better Way

This is multifaceted education, and it is the natural result of discussing great books and ideas—in all fields of learning, from literature to science, from math to history, from leadership to technology, and so on. To see how powerful it is, just compare this to the Lecture Method: You sit in class, a teacher talks about *Henry V*, you write down what he says so you'll be ready for the exam when it comes, you memorize the main points, and finally you take a test to see how well you remember what your teacher considered the main points. This methodology naturally teaches you *what* to think.

In contrast, the Discussion Model portrayed above very effectively teaches you *how* to think. Scholar Phase combines reading great books with discussing the great ideas they contain. This is the approach that birthed Oxford, Cambridge and the great universities and learning centers of Western Civilization, and also Asia. In fact, the masters of Asian learning usually approached education by asking lots of questions in what Westerners would call a very Socratic format.

Of course, it is possible to combine the discussion and lecture approaches with excellent results. Specifically: Attend a lecture by an expert with the same friends and parents, or other peers or mentors, then go to a restaurant or someone's living room and discuss what the lecturer taught. Or do the same thing with an online discussion group.

Again, use your notes. As everyone engages the topic and takes turns sharing what they learned from the lecture (agreed or disagreed with, and so on), you'll repeat the kind of amazing learning environment from the book club discussion I described previously.

But note clearly that it is the *discussion* about the lecture, not the lecture itself, and not even reading the book, that nearly always brings the most learning. In fact, try reading the lecturer's book before the lecture, then participating in a group discussion about what the speaker taught (both in her book and her lecture), and you'll have the best of multi-faceted learning. Still, the discussion is usually the most powerful learning environment of all those involved.

Mix and Match

In fact, even if you don't read the book, you'll frequently learn more from a good group discussion about the book than you would by reading the entire book on your own but never discussing it. The hierarchy of learning value is very real. In most cases:

- A lecture teaches you more than just eating popcorn or staring at the wall. Obviously.

- Reading teaches you more than attending a lecture.

- Reading *great* books sparks even more learning.

- Discussing with others teaches you more than just reading.

- Reading *and* discussing what you've read with others teaches you more than just discussing.

At a more advanced level:

- Reading and taking good margin notes, then discussing what you've learned with others who also read and took good margin notes, teaches you even more.

- Taking additional notes about what the members of such discussion groups share is even better.

- Reviewing such notes as you go through life, and adding to them as you re-read important books and ideas, is even better still.

If your reading doesn't excite you to the point that you have a bunch of important things you want to share with your friends, you're not reading the right things, or you need some practice reading the right way. Try the kind of note taking, followed by the kind of "group discussions", outlined above. Scholar Phase is all about reading the greatest books in multiple fields of learning, and reading them the right way: by turning all you read into great discussions with yourself, peers, and more advanced mentors.

If you struggle to really engage an inner dialogue with the author/book, you might benefit from hearing a group discussion from our online **TJEd High!** [TJEd.org/tjed-high] or **Mentoring in the Classics** [TJEd.org/MIC] series, where you can hear, feel and "taste" the experience vicariously in the voice and thoughts of youth who are really doing this.

Again, this works in all fields of learning, from literature, history, or philosophy to mathematics, science, technology, business, etc. The Discussion Method turns lower forms of learning into great learning.

Discussions with Mentors

Once you are routinely reading "the great way," by taking notes and engaging great authors in important conversations in margins throughout your books, and also having verbal, face-to-face, and written/texted/online discussions with your peers about truly great classics, it's time to engage great mentors as well. The quickest way to do this is to find out who the experts are on a topic and learn what they have to say.

But this can be a bit tricky. Why? Because to do this effectively, you aren't looking for merely *literary* or *academic* experts, you're looking for *successful* experts. The difference is significant. Find mentors who have excelled in the things you want to excel in. For example, years ago as a young married person I wanted to be the best husband I could become. To help myself improve, I researched the most popular books on marriage and started studying them. (In today's world, I would have included the best online tutorials as well.)

One day I mentioned this project to a class I was attending, and an older woman in the course began laughing. I couldn't see anything very funny about my comment, so I asked her what was up.

She apologized for finding my comments humorous, then said something I've never forgotten. "I studied those same books you just mentioned," she said, "until I found that they didn't work. Then I researched the authors and found that a number of them are not actually successful in marriage. They became experts on marriage academically, not through real-life personal success. And their book learning seldom actually works in the real world. I learned to only ask for marriage advice from people who have long, proven, great marriages. I've found that their suggestions are very, very different than the ideas found in most of those books."

After this conversation, I personally researched the books and authors to see if she was right, and it turns out she was. I returned those books to the library and began looking for people with great marriages. Over time I found that, yes, such people give very different marriage advice than any of those books—and it works.

I also learned a broader lesson from this experience. If you want to find the right mentor for something, look for someone who 1) loves the topic and 2) has succeeded in it—not necessarily someone with academic expertise on the topic. Such school-based expertise is often not very relevant to this type of education. Real success in a given field nearly always is.

The idea that "those who can't do, teach" is all well and good, except that learning things from those who have not only managed to do, but to be very successful at it, is an experience drastically different from the alternative. Those who have had to push through challenges and roadblocks again and again until they made it work have one main advantage over those who didn't: they actually *know* what works.

For example, if you want mentoring on entrepreneurial success and making money, find a mentor who has actually done it and done it well. Don't settle for someone who just has a certification, a degree, or who teaches classes on the topic. Academic expertise often falls far short of the real thing. The same is true with mentoring on healthy nutrition, getting in shape, getting a great education (and a great Scholar Phase), building better relationships, getting out of debt, learning to ride a horse, learning to skateboard, etc.

If you want quality mentoring that truly works, find mentors who have successfully accomplished what you want to achieve. There is frequently a huge gap between people who claim to be experts and those who have actually walked the walk. This lesson was reinforced for me one day when my martial arts instructor noticed I was holding my arm at a wrong angle during our training. He showed me several times what to do differently, but as soon as the class moved on he noticed that I reverted to my old way of doing things.

This happened several times, and eventually he halted the class and walked over to stand directly in front of me. He told me to hold my arm the way I had been holding it and that he was going to hit me. I agreed, and I went through the Karate move. He hit me, my arm buckled, and his fist drove into my gut. It really hurt. I mean, it really, really hurt.

"Ahhhh," I groaned. He smiled. "Now hold your arm the way I taught you," he said. I did it, and he hit me again. My arm blocked his, and it hardly hurt at all. "That's better," I said. He laughed. "Do it again," he told me. Then he hit me a lot harder. Then harder. Then even harder. Since I was holding my arm at the right angle, I easily and painlessly blocked every swing.

"Any questions?" he finally asked.

"No," I replied. From that point on I never again held my arm at the wrong angle.

This was a powerful lesson. To really learn effectively, especially from experts, we need to work with mentors who are actually good at the thing we're trying to learn. Forget their academic credentials—what are their real-life credentials? Can they walk the talk? If so, they are more likely to help you do the same.

Most often, parents are the best mentors. They are clearly committed, and they deeply care. They have more life experience than youth, and truly have so much to offer.

A Challenge

In terms of getting a great education and a quality Scholar Phase, a good mentor helps you see so many things in the classics you read and other experiences you have—things you typically won't see without the mentor's help. Permit me to illustrate.

Years ago I assigned *The Lord of the Flies* to a group of students I was mentoring. I had read it in high school, and I had a bad experience with it. The book was so dark, so devoid of hope. It created the impression of a world that is only selfishness, violence, and strife.

After I gained a quality Scholar Phase with the help of mentors who used the Discussion Method of great education, I went back to this book and re-read it. This time I saw much that I hadn't noticed the first time through. I realized that the author had actually taught the opposite of the lessons I once thought I found in the book—I had just been too intellectually unprepared to understand. I wanted my students to get this deeper, incredibly important message from the book, not the one I had erroneously learned in twelfth grade.

A few days after I gave the assignment, a father of one of my students called me. He was very disappointed that his daughter had been asked to read this particular book, and he was upset that I would even suggest it. He too had read it in high school, and had an experience very similar to my own.

I told him about my two very different experiences with the book, and suggested that with good mentoring his daughter would get something quite valuable from reading it. This made no sense to him. He was convinced that the book was what he had experienced—dark, selfish, devoid of hope, service and goodness—and that there was simply no other way to read the book.

I tried to tell him that the way mentors talk about a book has a huge impact on what students learn from it—but he just couldn't grasp what I meant. "The book is what it is," he kept saying. "You can't fix it or sugar coat it. I don't want my daughter to read it."

I told him that of course he and his daughter would have to make the final decision about her reading choices, but that mentoring makes all the difference on how a person experiences a book. This is the crux of the Discussion Method of learning. The discussion is the key, not the book. Again, he disagreed. Finally, he asked: "I've read *The Lord of the Flies*, and I hated it; if you were my mentor, how could you possibly make that any different?"

I was glad he at least wanted to understand my point of view, and I replied to his question with a few Socratic-style questions. They went something like this: "In so many ways, *The Lord of the Flies* is like our current world, don't you agree?"

"Well, in the bad ways, yes."

"Like what?"

"Well, like people caring only about themselves, and hating and hurting anyone who is different, and banding together in power groups to control others. And killing those who try to teach morality or goodness. And using violence as their first resort, way too often. It's just sick…"

"I agree," I responded. "But *should* our world be that way?"

"Of course not!"

"How should it be different? Specifically, how should the boys on the island have done things differently?"

"Well…" he pondered. "They should have done everything differently. Everything."

"Okay. Let's get specific. They started out by organizing, choosing leaders, and making sure everyone had food and water. Was that bad?"

"Well, no. They started off okay, I guess."

"Then at what point did they go wrong?"

"I…I'm not sure. I don't remember every detail. Just that it turned out so sick."

"Yes, it did. But why? Why did it turn out sick? What happened that led the boys to such a sick and selfish society?"

Long silence. "Well, at some point they started killing each other."

"Just like in the real world, right?"

"Yes! Exactly…" More silence.

"Can I tell you what I think?" I asked respectfully.

"Sure. Please do."

"I think *The Lord of the Flies* is a book about what happens in the world when human beings follow their own paths, rather than following God and morals. I think the author knew this, and that the island in the book was just a metaphor of the earth. When we as human beings follow God and his moral code, it doesn't turn out like the story on the island. But when we reject the moral code, it gets really bad. Really ugly."

I paused. He was silent. Then, slowly, he said, "That's really true. That's exactly what the book shows."

I started to say more, but he interrupted me: "But I don't think the author did that on purpose, like you say he did. The book shows how our world has become one big Lord of the Flies because people don't live a decent moral code. But that's just coincidence. I think the author was actually trying to promote such a world. That's why the book ends up so sick and violent."

"I don't think so," I replied. "You know why?"

"Why?"

"Do you remember how the book ends?"

"Uh, yes. The kids are rescued."

"Right. Do you remember who rescues them?"

"A ship, right?"

"Yes. But what kind of ship?"

Silence. "I don't remember."

"It was a war ship. The rescuers were on their way to bomb, kill, and destroy the enemy. They interrupted the mob of boys hunting down a boy to kill him—but after they rescued the kids and got them all on the ship, the ship's commanders returned to their real mission: to hunt down the enemy and kill them."

Long silence.

"What's the message of such a story?" I asked.

This time the father's voice was totally different. It was now animated, excited. "It's what you said before. The book is about how our world has totally gotten off track, all because we've forgotten the moral code and we're just focused on fighting, winning, and selfish goals. That's awesome! The sickness of the book shows just how sick our modern world is! The sickness in the book is no different than watching the sickness on the nightly news…but almost nobody realizes it…"

He stopped talking, out of breath.

"Don't you think our young people should understand this message?" I asked. "Not six-year-olds, of course. Or even ten-year-olds. But your daughter is older than that. Don't you think this would help her education?"

"Absolutely!" he said. Then he surprised me. "Can I attend your discussion?" he asked. "I've hated that book since high school, but I really think I need to learn what you're teaching about it."

"Well, I'm not so much teaching as discussing it," I told him. I invited him to come, and everyone involved that day had a great discussion. But the whole experience taught me something very important—or reinforced it, actually. Mentors make a huge difference in how we understand a book.

It's not the book. It's the discussion. This is the hidden secret of truly great education. That's why many elite prep schools provide a much higher-quality education than most public schools. It's discussion. It makes a huge difference.

Does the book matter? Yes, of course. That's why the great classics are so important. But the book matters primarily as a starting place for great mentoring, and for great discussions—starting with your personal notes in the margins.

Reframing it All

Another example: When I read Shakespeare's *Romeo and Juliet* in school I found it very disappointing. Everyone died at the end, nothing was solved, nothing got better, and nobody improved. "What was the point?" I wondered. And no mentor gave me any answers.

Years later, after learning from Scholar Phase mentors how to really discuss a book—with self and others—I read the same play again and it made incredible sense—profound sense. In fact, it is one of the most important classics I've ever read. But without the Discussion Method of learning, I would never have realized it.

I think a lot of people who read *Romeo and Juliet* in schools based on the Lecture Method had the same experience. So let's reframe it right now, using the Discussion Method.

*** [Spoiler Alert] ***

Specifically, *Romeo and Juliet* teaches a very important principle—one that is key to life success, leadership, and happiness. The turning point of the play comes when Romeo learns that Juliet is dead and has to make a decision. Up to this point in the story, Romeo has followed the advice of his Friar, who has been helping him find a way to marry Juliet even though both of their families hate each other and hate the idea of these two young people getting married.

The Friar has a plan, and it is a pretty good one. It had every chance of working. But Romeo doesn't know the whole plan, he has just been relying on his trust of the Friar. When he hears the report that Juliet is dead, he finds himself at a crossroads. He can keep trusting the Friar (who symbolically stands for God), or he can reject "heaven's" plan and take matters into his own hands. But at this point it all seems hopeless to him.

He loves Juliet, and if he would have followed the Friar's plan, things would likely have worked out "happily ever after" (she isn't actually dead)—with more support from both families. But he doesn't. In his grief and anger, he shakes his fist at heaven and says the fateful words: "I defy you, stars."

In other words, "I'm not going with heaven's plan. Forget God! I'm going to take matters into my own hands." He decides that doing things your own way, and according to your own wisdom, is the best way to get what you want in this life. It appears to him that he has lost what he loved most by following God's plan, and he now turns against it. *Following heaven's way doesn't work*, Romeo has decided.

Note that there is a significant difference between how most people see priests, friars, pastors or other church leaders and heaven in modern times versus the way the Shakespearean audiences understood this. But without getting into the cultural differences, we can still learn a lot from the story. (In a longer discussion, such historical differences would add to the quality of learning. For example, the difference between priests, monks, friars, pastors, etc., is very interesting.)

In short, Romeo turns from the path (following the Friar's plan, symbolically heaven's plan) that would have brought him the wife he loved and all he hoped for, and instead takes the fork in the road that leads to the loss of all he cares about—including his own life and that of the woman he loves.

Bad decision.

Yet Shakespeare uses the story to teach us one of the greatest lessons of human life. Trust heaven. Follow the right path, the path of the good, the true, the moral. Don't trust in your own power and force what you want. Might isn't right. Not at all. Choose the righteous way, and choose the right—even if it's scary or seems uncertain. God's moral code—taught in very similar words in all the great world religions and philosophies, as C.S. Lewis pointed out in detail in *The Abolition of Man*—is the way to happiness. Stick with it, even when things seem difficult or too hard. Do the right thing to the best of your understanding and ability. Always.

Shakespeare's message is powerful. And in this case he taught it through a love story, which was genius—because affairs of the heart are one place where people may be the most likely to compromise their principles. But to see the deeper meaning, we need to know how to "discuss" what we read—especially with ourselves. If no mentor helps us see the hidden messages, then we need to be able to at least understand how a mentor would question, probe and discuss the things we read—so we can do the same in our own mind as we're learning. Knowing how to take the right kind of handwritten margin notes drastically improves this ability.

Real Reading

Beyond these examples from *The Lord of the Flies* and the writings of Shakespeare, the Discussion Method of learning helps us automatically read with this kind of depth—whatever we're reading. This works. It is the skill of true *thinking* education, and *true* reading. Those who know how to do it read the same things as other people, but get so much *more* out of what they read—so, so much more!

Indeed, throughout history the wealthy classes have typically trained their youth to read and think this way, while the lower classes haven't. In fairness, many in the middle and lower classes didn't even know how to do this—had little concept of it—making it difficult for them to pass it on to their youth. The truth is that most people still don't know how to read this way even in today's world. It is seldom taught—except among the upper classes, or others who get a Scholar Phase. This one thing, more than any other, is responsible for the huge class divisions that different types of education perpetuate in modern society.

Lewis Carroll provided several examples of this disconnect in his classic children's book, *Alice in Wonderland*. But the book isn't really for children at all. It is full of deep symbolism that only a mature mind can clearly understand. Young adults get it, if they know how to truly think while they're reading. The most effective, and easiest, way to teach this is through discussion. Again, the elite classes teach this kind of thinking and reading through discussion of great books and ideas. Most other people don't.

The result is a kind of disconnected language — the upper classes understand the same words and phrases to mean different things than do the middle and lower classes. Carroll pointed this out with misunderstandings like the following:

> "Mine is a long and a sad tale!" said the Mouse, turning to Alice and sighing.
>
> "It is a long tail, certainly," said Alice, looking down with wonder at the Mouse's tail, "but why do you call it sad?"

Carroll portrays Alice as a representative of the middle and lower classes who keeps running into aristocrats — whose words she can't quite seem to grasp. Another example:

> "If everyone minded their own business," the Duchess said in a hoarse growl, "the world would go round a great deal faster than it does."

The aristocratic lady means, of course, that the world would be a better place and people would get along much more amiably. Alice, however, hears the same words, but only understands their literal meaning:

> "Which would not be an advantage," said Alice …. "Just think what work it would make with the day and the night! You see the earth takes twenty-four hours to turn round on its axis—"

The Duchess sees exactly what Alice is lacking, and immediately throws it right back at her:

> "Talking of axes," said the Duchess, "chop off her head!"

On an even deeper level, Carroll shows us that what means one thing to the upper class doesn't mean the same to the masses. The Cheshire Cat tells Alice:

> "...a dog growls when it's angry, and wags its tail when it's pleased. Now I growl when I'm pleased and wag my tail when I'm angry."

The point is that different classes understand the same words very differently. But Alice misses the powerful symbolism—proving the Cat's point. Her education is still stuck on the literal, lower-class level. She replies:

> "I call it purring, not growling."

Alexis de Tocqueville addressed this very topic in *Democracy in America* when he wrote about the differences between the people of America and the upper classes in Europe. He noted that all education in America emphasizes things that are practical and useful, without much regard for the symbolic, beautiful, or profound. As he put it, "[Americans] habitually prefer the useful to the beautiful, and they ... require that the beautiful will be useful."[13]

"Why are Americans this way?" he wondered. Because hard work was the universal American pastime and the American way. Working people tend to care mostly about practical things, not the abstract or symbolic. The value of this is that even more work gets done. But it also puts such people at a disadvantage to the elite classes, whose education teaches them to notice details and nuances that most of the regular people don't even see—like Alice.

The real-life result is that over time the practical American middle class lost much of its influence and control over the nation. This power shifted to the more subtle elite classes, and it is still flowing to them today. In other words, the education and lifestyle gap between those who are taught as young people that success comes from listening and following (the Lecture Method) and their "privileged" peers educated as independent thinkers and innovative leaders (the Discussion Method) is very wide.

In short: the Discussion Approach to education is vital to great learning. This is one of the most practical and useful truths in all of modern education, career, and life. Specifically, nearly *everything* we read can be great if we know *how* to read (and think) greatly. Or, in other words, if

---

13 Alexis de Tocqueville, *Democracy in America*, vol. 2, p. 48 (Vintage Classics edition, Henry Reeve, Phillips Bradley)

we are holding a powerful discussion in our mind with everything we study and read. This is the crux of real reading, and of great education. Discussion matters! And it directly impacts the quality of education (and prosperity level) of families and individuals who either learn this skill… or not.

Scholar Phase and the 9 Skills are essential.

When the Student is Ready…

So, on a practical level, how can you apply the lesson of getting the right mentor(s) for an excellent Scholar Phase that teaches you the 9 Skills?[14] First of all, let's get very clear about what you are actually looking for. The most important part of learning in Scholar Phase is to be able to recognize and learn great and meaningful lessons while reading the great books or learning in any other way. To do this, an effective mentor needs enough wisdom and life experience to see how what happens in books relates directly to you and your life, and enough love and care for you to help you see it.

Again, for most youth, nobody does these things better than parents. Period.

This is a big deal. While your parents may help you find additional coaches, tutors, mentors, classes, or peer groups, your parent is usually the best mentor to help you get the most effective personal learning from great classics. Clearly a few parents don't want to, or, for various reasons, are limited in their ability to fill this role—but many (hopefully most) can. But no matter their limitations, have the wisdom and humility to learn from them—because they do have much to offer, whether or not it is obvious to them or to you. Wherever possible, start with your parents as your most powerful mentors in Scholar Phase.

This is simple—for you, and for your parent. Simply agree to read a great book at the same time, and then discuss the book together. Talk about what you learn, what you like and dislike, any questions that arise, and whatever else comes to mind.

---

14   See the Note to Readers at the beginning of the book.

To help youth and parents experience first-hand how this process actually works in real life, we put together several years' worth of such discussions (one book per month, or at your own pace) called the **Mentoring in the Classics** program. These are available as easy-to-access online audios and study guides via subscription at TJEd.org/MIC.

You can get these fun audios and listen to them in your own home or car, and they include real parents and youth discussing many great classics—one per month for over four years. It's like a reality show about Scholar Phase, and you can follow our children as they progress from just-getting-started, with their earnest first efforts at discussing at an adult level, and see them come into their own over the course of the months and years, with a mentored scholar phase and effective discussions with family and mentors.

People who participate in this service often comment about the epiphanies they get, and how, with the benefit of hearing multiple discussions among parents and their youth, they finally "get it." They quickly internalize just how to have such great discussions themselves. They learn how to effectively get great education, because it is modeled for them. By the time you have read three or four books and listened to the youth/mentor discussion audios about each of them, you'll start to feel like you have what you need to do this yourself (whether you're a parent or a youth). By the time you've listened to seven or eight of these book discussions, you'll feel like a veteran.

Reading great books and discussing them effectively is the key to great education. The better the discussions, the better and deeper the learning.

Putting it All Together

The truth is that a large proportion of youth who get a great Scholar Phase have at least one parent who has already done a Scholar Phase, or who is actively progressing in the phase that they are in—whatever it may be. Parents have the life experience and wisdom to give some of the best personalized mentoring to each young person, and when they read and discuss the great books with their youth everyone experiences a whole new level of truly great education.

The discussions youth and parents have about great books and other great works and ideas are, literally, priceless. They are the essence of Scholar Phase, and the DNA of any truly great education—wherever it takes place, and whatever it is called. It is possible to replicate this system between non-parent mentors and students (which is what colleges and universities were originally created to accomplish), but the ideal is often most effectively achieved when a parent actively participates in this process.

Indeed, the discussions that take place when parents (and other mentors) engage the great books and ideas with their youth are the most important part of all education. To the extent that you make this part of your family culture, you are passing on truly great education, and legacy, to your children. This is the type of education that naturally and effectively helps each young person master the 9 Skills.

Again, for any parent who worries that he/she isn't quite ready to do this, the "Mentoring in the Classics" audios make it truly simple and easy. The beginning of a truly great education is just a few classics away—for anyone. Engaging this process together as parent and youth is powerful, simple, and incredibly effective.

But whether you use the TJEd.org audios or not, great education thrives when a parent and youth read great books and discuss them—over and over. Nothing else measures up. Nothing else even comes close.

Indeed, part of the Internet revolution is that today the kind of top-tier great education once reserved for the children of royalty and the super-rich is now available to every parent, every child, every youth, in every home. Great education, and a great Scholar Phase, can help each person—young and old—achieve his best life and fulfill his unique life mission and life purpose. Each person has greatness within. The role of great education is to help unlock that greatness and unleash it in the world.

Such a process is seldom easy or immediate. A great education takes a lot of effort, work, and learning. But getting a truly excellent Scholar Phase is simple for those who put in the work: read the greatest books from all fields of knowledge, and engage lots of discussion with yourself, peers, and mentors.

The right kind of discussions, as outlined in this chapter (and modeled in the "Mentoring in the Classics" audios), are essential to great education and learning *how* to truly think—and apply your thinking, knowledge and skills. The stakes are high, because this type of learning unleashes the best kind of quality education. Yet the process is simple, as shown. In fact, it is much simpler than most educational bureaucracies want anyone to realize. The Discussion Method is incredibly effective. It naturally leads to great education, great career, great impact.

Perhaps the very best news is simply this: Every youth can do it. And so can every parent. Starting now. The beginning of a great education is just a discussion away.

A Secret

One of the most challenging impediments to a successful Scholar Phase comes from an unexpected place. Because this generation of parents has little or no experience with Scholar Phase as a youth, we really don't conceive of the amount of emotional energy and actual time necessary to successfully engage with this kind of study. Society doesn't reward it, social relationships militate against it… and then, right in the home, the parents tend to create incessant interruptions, chores, competing messages, and habits that interfere with the Scholar's success.

But there is a secret to help guard against these anti-Scholar Phase pressures! To learn more about how to empower Scholar Phase, and the "8 Common Mistakes" parents make with regard to Scholar Phase, read chapter 7 of *The Phases of Learning* (by Oliver and Rachel DeMille).

3
The Mini-Workshop

*"I know who I was when I got up this morning,
but I think I must have…changed several times since then."*
–ALICE IN WONDERLAND

*"O excellent device! Was there ever heard a better?—That my master,
being scribe, to himself should write the letter."*
–SHAKESPEARE

THE purpose of this chapter is to start changing the way you read. I'm going to make this as easy as possible, so that every reader starts developing deeper reading skills. This will be very basic, not complicated at all. But it is also very effective. All you have to do is read the chapter and answer the questions. Answer them in writing. Note that the questions aren't difficult; in fact, they're actually fun.

That's it. The reading and answering (which is a form of discussion when you write down your answers) will put you on the track of great reading.

There are only a few short exercises in these workshops. I recommend you do each of them, and have fun with them. I hope you won't skip anything in this chapter. Getting these skills is vital for Scholar Phase (and for teaching Scholar Phase). While the exercises are simple, they are powerful. You'll be different when you've completed them.

Workshop #1: Answer the *Alice in Wonderland* Questions

In this enjoyable classic by Lewis Carroll, young Alice jumps down a rabbit hole and ends up experiencing a number of adventures. As she travels from place to place in Wonderland, meeting many different characters, she faces a series of very important questions. Indeed, they are some of the most important questions any of us face in life. Carroll created a masterpiece, all built around the truth that asking and effectively answering a few key questions is one of the real purposes of life. If we do it well, we'll experience more success, progress, and happiness.

There are only five of these questions, but they are very important. Answer each of the following questions (the same ones Alice faced) in your own handwriting:

A. Who do you want to become in your life? Seriously. Who
     and what do you want to be? (It's okay if you change your
     mind later. Just write what you think your answer is now.)

B. What do you love the very most?

C. Where will your life most likely end up if
     you continue on your current path?

D. What should you stop pretending to be in life?

E. What is the biggest single change you
     should make right now in your life?

Workshop #2: Reading the Little Things

Just consider the different meanings of the following sentences:

- **I** didn't say the man was big.

- I **didn't** say the man was big.

- I didn't **say** the man was big.

- I didn't say **the** man was big.

- I didn't say the **man** was big.

- I didn't say the man **was** big.

- I didn't say the man was **big**.

Each sentence has a very different meaning. We can go even deeper with this:

- I didn't say "the man" was big.
  (The CEO of my company isn't big.)

- I didn't—say, the man was big.
  (The speaker starts to say something, then stops
  and exclaims how big someone is.)

- I didn't say, "The man was big."
  (Same as: I didn't *say* the man was big.)

- I didn't. Say: "The man was big."
  (I did not. That's final. Now, new thought, I want
  you to say these words: "The man was big.")

That's ten different meanings in eleven sentences, using exactly the same words in the same order. In other words, it's important to read closely. Different punctuation and emphasis really do change the meaning of things.

This exercise is done. Just by reading it closely your brain has made a change—you'll realize that little details in what you read can make a big difference, and you'll start noticing such details more frequently.

Workshop #3: The Tiny Switch

Our brains need to learn to see things differently, and to compare the differences. It doesn't take much to turn on this part of our brains, but a lot of people never really do so. We're going to accomplish this very quickly and easily. Just read the following quotes, all from *Alice in Wonderland*:

Twinkle, twinkle, little bat!

How I wonder what you're at.

Now, notice several things.

First: this verse says nothing about stars, but you probably have the word "star" in your mind.

Second: this verse provides no musical notes or bars, but you likely have the tune to "Twinkle, Twinkle, Little Star" in your mind.

This is an example of having a discussion with yourself—your mind filling in thoughts, ideas, references, and other things all on its own. The author didn't tell you anything about a star, or suggest a melody—but your mind provides them anyway. This is natural discussion with yourself as you read.

Your mind also probably knows that the tune you just hummed with "twinkle, twinkle" is the same one used with "The Alphabet Song." Remember: "A, B, C, D, E, F, G…" But have you ever consciously noticed that the two songs utilize the same tune? No doubt your subconscious mind caught this connection.

In fact, your mind is so good at filling things in and making surprising connections that it will even disagree with what it reads when it sees something wrong. For example, read the next quote below.

Alice said: "Let me see, four times five is twelve, and four times six is thirteen…. London is the capital of Paris, and Paris is the capital of Rome, and Rome—no, that's all wrong…"

Alice is wrong on every point. But your mind probably caught the mistakes as you read, right? Carroll wrote it this way, I believe, to make sure readers would realize the mistakes and slow down and read wisely. Deeply. The way people with a great education read.

To be specific: people with a great education read in a *thinking* way, so if something the author says is wrong, or seems to be wrong, or if there are even possible alternatives that could be better, they stop and think about it. On the other hand, people without a great education tend to read to get the "right" answer (memorize what the writer has said), without really questioning the author's words.

Carroll makes sure every reader *thinks* while reading his book. Not all authors do that, of course. Almost none do it. But Carroll is teaching us to really think and internally discuss ideas as we read — the key to a great education. This teaches us the 9 Skills naturally as we read.

This kind of reading is powerful. In fact, your thinking mind not only naturally picks out flaws as it reads, it also draws pictures. The next quote illustrates how this works.

"There's no use in knocking," said the footman, "…because I'm on the same side of the door as you…"

Read that again, to be sure you understand it. Once you grasp what's happening, your mind draws a picture: Both Alice and the footman standing in front of a door, looking at a door together. Note that the words don't provide a drawing, nor do the words describe a scene in detail. But for most people, your thinking mind knows how to turn words into images, and vice versa. For those that find this doesn't come naturally, rest assured that it does get easier!

We could continue with many more examples, but we've already achieved what is needed. With some effort and attention ("mindfulness"), your mind will naturally start to notice such tiny switches from now on, and you'll get better at it as you practice noticing such details more often. But even if you do nothing about it, your mind already knows how to do it. For example:

Mary had a little…

Happy birthday to…

For he's a jolly good…

What happens in Vegas…

Your mind fills in so much beyond the words, all on its own. When you don't just ignore this, but actually focus on doing it a lot, your mind is discussing what it is reading and you're engaging higher-level thinking. In fact, in the case of the "what happens in Vegas" quote, your mind not only fills in extra words but probably also finds itself disagreeing with the quote! See, you are discussing things you read all the time—often without realizing it.

Workshop #4: Learn About Phantom Tollbooth-Style Questions

In the classic book *The Phantom Tollbooth*, the main character Milo goes on a journey of the mind. In the story, he embarks on a long trip, but symbolically the message is that he really just started reading a good book—and it took him on a journey of learning.

In the process, he learns to ask and answer a certain type of question. To learn the same skill, answer the following questions in writing:

1. Is the Milky Way Galaxy big or small?
   (This is a strange question, but do your best to answer
   it anyway. And relax: there's no test, no grade. It's
   just a thinking exercise. Have fun. Enjoy!)

2. Does an ant running as fast as it can move quickly or slowly?
   (Again, strange question. Just give it your best shot, and
   write down your answers. [Note: it's okay to have one
   answer, or two, twenty-five, or whatever you choose.])

3. Is a 5-inch cube of steel best described as solid or hollow?

4. Is a car most accurately described as light or heavy?

The answer to all these questions is the same: "It depends." The Milky Way isn't the biggest or the smallest galaxy, so its size depends on what you compare it to. It is bigger than your house, but much smaller than the universe. An ant is moving a lot faster than a stationary kitchen table, but the ant is also probably on a planet that is moving pretty quickly around the sun, and in a galaxy that is hurtling at high speed through space. Likewise, to a dog, a 5-inch cube of steel is pretty solid, but to a subatomic particle such as a neutrino or a quark, the same cube of steel contains more space than matter.

In other words, the answer to all these questions is simply "It depends." This kind of thinking is important, because our modern school system often teaches us not to even consider thinking this way. "What is 2 + 2?" we are asked, and expected to always answer "4". But is there no other possible answer? In most math classes, there probably isn't. But in leadership, the concept of synergy is that 2 + 2 can equal 5, or 18, or some other number where the sum is greater than the parts.

Indeed, in highly advanced mathematics 2 + 2 seldom equals 4 because you have to account for the quality of the item, not just the quantity of 2. To make this very simple, the number 2 is equal to another number 2, but 2 apples are almost never equal to 2 oranges. In fact, no 2 oranges are equal to any other 2 oranges. Yes, they have the same numerical "unit" value on paper. But beyond this they are different in many ways—sometimes in big ways, and other times in very small ways.

It is important to be able to think in multiple ways: both 2 + 2 = 4, and any 2 oranges won't be equal to any other 2 oranges. All of this might seem abstract, because it is. But learning to read and discuss, and to really think, means being able to understand the abstract along with the literal, and to recognize the difference.

There. We're done with this for now. But, assuming you didn't already think in multiple ways before you read this, your brain has experienced a change.

Workshop #5: The Important Thing is to be a Great Reader

Great learning is less about reading great things, and more about reading greatly—about becoming a great reader. Great readers can learn from almost anything: technical manuals, textbooks, and even billboards, memes, or marketing ads.

You want to become the kind of reader who learns great things even from mediocre writings. When you're good at this, just imagine how much you'll learn from truly great writings. Great writings + great reader + lots of discussions = truly great education. That's what we're aiming for. The key is to really look for deep and important meaning—whatever we're reading—and anything that can help us improve ourselves, and our lives.

Let's practice doing this. To begin this process, a motto used in many marketing ads by the prestigious Patek Philippe watch company is really powerful:

**"You never actually own
a Patek Philippe.**

**"You merely take care of it for
the next generation."**

This is often presented along with the additional tagline:

"Build Your Own Tradition"

For me, this teaches a poignant lesson about every great classic book you and I ever read, write in, and pass on to the next generation. This is deep.

Think about it. When you read a great book and write in the margins like we discussed in the last chapter (ideas, disagreements, references to other books that teach similar concepts, ?, !, highlighting, underlining, circling, etc.) you add your voice to the great debate and the great conversation of human history. And every time you re-read the same classic, you can add additional handwritten notes, thoughts, and ideas. All it takes is a pen.

By doing this, over time, you build on the shoulders of giants, starting with a great work like *Les Miserables*, the *Federalist Papers, Pride and Prejudice*, etc. and adding more thoughts. When you pass such a volume on to your posterity (who have been educated in the greats and know how to engage an on-going dialogue with every book they read, as well as with the handwritten notes they are thrilled to discover in the margins), you give them a mighty treasure.

Indeed: A great classic with your notes in it is an even *greater* classic.

That's worth stitching into a sign for the wall, or etching into marble, or posting on every possible social media site. Let's read it again:

> A great classic with your notes in it is
> an even *greater* classic.

Here are several other famous marketing slogans that have relevant messages for quality education. As you read each, focus on what the words could mean to your education and any other part of your life right now. Write your thoughts of how to personally use each message in the space provided:

- Live Each Day As If It's The Only One (Dove ad)

- Only Those Who Dare Drive the World Forward (Cadillac ad)

- Created to Serve (TIAA ad)

- Put Good In, You Get Good Out (Minute Maid ad)

- Let's Go Places (Toyota ad)

- BINGE-READING: It's About To Be A Thing (Texture ad)

- Remember the Moment; Forget the Mess (Libman ad)

- Relax (Tommy Bahama ad)

- Ask Questions (Charles Schwab ad)

- Start the Conversation
  (I think it is significant that this slogan is found in ads
  from Doubleday, the book publisher. After all, the Great
  Conversation frequently begins with books.)

- The Love of Reading (Kindle ad)

Some of these slogans are really powerful. Translating them to the specific needs of your life can be profound. It allows you to turn the ad into real learning and personal improvement. Reading and applying things this way leads to wisdom. In fact, on a broader scale, try looking for such meaning in everything you read.

Now, go back through the above list and circle or highlight the one or two that you think could most benefit you right now. This is very important discussion—when it reaches the level of practical, real-life application.

By the way, the large majority (a super majority!) of ads I came across while researching this topic were static (e.g. "Available At [some website]" or "15% Savings on…"). Kind of like a conveyor-belt school of ads. Not very inspiring.

But I found a few that were really worth thinking about. For example, one ad struck me as particularly great for young people, homeschoolers, and also committed parents, teachers, mentors and learners:

For The Pioneer In You (Montblanc ad)

This really gets to the heart of things. Truly great education is an act of pioneering, of blazing trails. Another excellent ad, which certainly pertains to great education, is:

Anyone Can Change Everything (Rolex ad)

Perhaps the best, most inspiring ad I read was very simple, not complex. Yet it contains one of the great Core Phase messages of life:

The Power of Hugs (Huggies ad)

Like I said, it's simple, but incredibly genuine. Just like most great classics. Again, apply this motto: Who needs more hugs in your life? How can you help with this? Do you hug your parents enough? Parents, do you hug your teens enough? Enough hugs can make all the difference—in learning, relationships, and in the other facets of life. (Of course, don't try this in a public school setting. It's best reserved for home!)

Here's an ad slogan that really speaks to getting a great education by reading the best books and taking good handwritten notes in them—for yourself, and for later generations. This excellent motto from BIC pens unabashedly gets it right:

Handwriting Sparks Creativity

When reading a great book, or anything else, get out your pen and make a classic even better. If you aren't sure what to write in the margins, just write brief questions about what you're reading. Not only does this kind of learning improve the book for the next reader, but taking the time to formulate and articulate your thoughts and questions in handwritten margin notes also increases the quality and depth of what you learn from each book. It's the first discussion you'll have with every book.

Great learning comes from great reading, and great reading means a dialogue between you and the author—and discussions with others. When you write in a book in the right way, you are boosting great learning for yourself and everyone else who has the good fortune of reading the book with your notes in the margins. Great education is always interactive, participative. Again, this makes a great classic into an even greater book. Apply the same principles to everything you read: always be on the lookout for any great or helpful ideas you can learn.

Why It Matters

Hopefully the simple workshops in this chapter were at least a little bit fun for you. If nothing else, your analytical and thinking centers are now warmed up and ready for action. With this in place, we are now ready to move on to the specifics of Scholar Phase (the 21st Century replacement to the 20th Century high school): what to do, and how to do it.

BOOK TWO

"LIGHTS, CAMERA, ACTION!"

"To know and not to do,
is not to know."

–LEO BUSCAGLIA

4

The Practice Year

T HE old-style education system that rules most of our current schools is behind the times. Outdated. Quaint. Sadly, it is still preparing students for the kind of jobs that were plentiful in the 1960s, but less so in the 1990s, and increasingly scarce today. We need education for the 21st Century, education that will prepare us for the economy of our time and the decades ahead, for the emerging era of entrepreneurship and innovation. On top of this, we have children and youth in the world who were born to make a meaningful contribution, and they will need the kind of broad, deep, and *great* education that will prepare them for it. In short, we need Scholar Phase. And soon…

By this point in the book, you know at least three things that are very important. First, getting a great Scholar Phase is the key to a truly great education. Second, the way to get a great Scholar Phase is to read great books on many topics and do a lot of quality discussion about them. Third, it is easy to learn how to effectively discuss great books—simply listen to 5-6 of the Mentoring in the Classics audios and learn how it is done in a family setting, or get some kind of similar experience with a great mentor; or, alternatively, join TJEd High! for a youth-centered experience.

When you apply these things, you are on the path of truly great education—for you, your youth, and everyone else in your family. Once you are doing the three things mentioned above, the rest of getting a great Scholar Phase is simple.

But one important question remains: What does Scholar Phase look like beyond reading great books and participating in quality discussions, and how does it unfold year to year? Let's get specific in addressing these questions.

The Map

Scholar Phase is a 3-5 year process for a teen or youth (because most teens have time to read and discuss for many hours a day, if they choose), and a bit longer process for working adults. (Our best advice for adults doing Scholar Phase is to enroll in the Mentoring in the Classics program—TJEd. org/MIC.)

The measure of Scholar Phase isn't really in years, however, but in hours. A quality Scholar Phase takes approximately 5,000 hours for most people—but it can be accomplished with a bit less or may need a bit more. As we've already mentioned, the 5,000 hours are spent directly reading great books in various fields of knowledge and discussing them (verbally and/or in writing). If you're counting hours reading and discussion hour for hour, be advised that sitting in class listening to lectures doesn't count for the same hour-value.

The 3-5 years break down as follows:

Year 1   Practice Year

Year 2   Intense Reading Year 1

Year 3   Intense Reading Year 2

Year 4   Intense Reading Year 3 and The Class

Year 5   Intense Reading Year 4 and The Bridge

Again, some students will complete this in less than 5 years. Others may want to pursue a more leisurely pace. It is important for students to go at a pace that feels best to them—rather than trying to fit some external agenda. The goal is great learning, not checking off bureaucratic boxes or meeting some arbitrary deadline (the eighteenth birthday is a common one, for example).

Those who complete 5,000 hours of reading great books and greatly discussing them in 3 years, for example, will likely add The Class in Year 2 and The Bridge in Year 3. And the Practice Year may only last a few months for such accelerated (often natural literary-style) learners.

Personalization is the name of the game. If a student loves learning and is actively reading and discussing the greats, he or she is on track. A 5- or even 6-year pace is just as good as a 3- or 4-year approach, depending on the needs of each student. To repeat: *Personalize the program to the needs of each student.* The objective is for each individual to get a great education—not meet some externally-determined time standard.

With that said, let's look at how the Practice Year shakes out. This is very important, because too many parents and/or students try to get the student to do too much during this year—and as a result they don't experience a true Practice Year, and veer off track before the course even begins in earnest. Doing this well really matters.

Year 1

The Practice Year is a very important part of Scholar Phase. It may last a year, or only a few months—or even 18 months or two years. For many students who begin scholar phase in a "normal" fashion as they experience the changes of puberty, a year is just right. Older students, or those with a natural learning style other than "literary" may work effectively with a different pace or timeline. But however long the individual student chooses to be a Practice Scholar, he or she will be reading great classics and discussing them (in all three ways outlined in Chapter 2).

The difference between the Practice Year and the later Intense Reading Years is that Practice Scholars simply *play* at the process. It isn't their fulltime job or focus, but rather a part-time hobby. They'll try it out, like trying on clothes at the mall. They'll date it, not quite marry it yet. They dip their foot in the water, so to speak, learn what they like and don't like, and build an aptitude and appetite for the hard work of study.

It really is this simple.

To begin Scholar Phase, don't leap into the deepest part of the lake without testing the water. Just put your toe in at first. Check out the temperature. Stick in your finger. See what you think.

That's Year 1.

The First Step

Read a great book. Practice taking the kind of notes discussed in Chapter 2. Attend a discussion about the book — in person, or online. Organize such a discussion if needed. Discuss with a parent(s), a sibling(s), or a friend(s). Or all three. You can also discuss the great book with some other small group. You'll need at least two people to do this, and 4-7 is probably ideal. More than 15 means most of the participants won't get the opportunity to say very much, and the quieter ones will feel no pressure or motivation to speak up at all — so fewer is often better. Or, if you're participating in an online discussion group, a lot of learners can effectively take part.

A little sidebar: While there is great merit in actively participating in a discussion, be aware that not all learn by speaking. Quiet people can gain a great deal from the process as well. And while quiet ones do well to challenge themselves to speak up a little more than they're comfortable with, those who usually have a lot to say often do just as well to challenge themselves to speak a little less and listen more effectively and with more earnest intent to hear and understand another's thoughts.

Once you've taken this first step and participated in a book discussion, talk it over with your parent(s). What did you like about the discussion experience? What didn't you like very much?

Here are some recommended books to choose from for your first read:

The Great Brain (Fitzgerald)

The Cricket in Times Square (Seldon and Williams)

Pawn of Prophecy (Eddings)

The Phantom Tollbooth (Juster)

Carry On, Mr. Bowditch (Latham)

Trumpet of the Swan (White)

Little Women (Alcott)

Little Men (Alcott)

Anne of Green Gables (Montgomery)

Tom Sawyer (Twain)

The Lion, the Witch, and the Wardrobe (Lewis)

Little House in the Big Woods (Wilder)

Pollyanna (Porter)

Thomas Jefferson Education for Teens (DeMille and Brooks)

Turn the Page (Brady)

The Five Love Languages of Teenagers (Chapman)

Archimedes and the Door of Science (Bendick)

Spiritual Lives of the Great Composers (Kavanaugh)

Say*Go*Be*Do (Earl)

Do Hard Things (Harris and Harris)

The Declaration of Independence

Here There Be Dragons (Owen)

"Give Me Liberty or Give Me Death" (Henry)

The Inner Ring (Lewis)

Don't be limited to this list. Look through the books in your home, and at the library. And look up the books (on the list above) on Amazon or Goodreads and see what other books are recommended for people who liked them.

Of course, different people are at differing reading levels at the beginning of the Practice Year—so pick a book that seems right for you. The best way to do this is to pick up the book and read a few random passages. If it seems interesting and is easy to understand, great. If not, search for one that is. If you are finding your books online, Amazon frequently allows you to preview books and read a few parts of the book before you commit to reading the whole thing.

Now, as outlined, read a book, take lots of handwritten notes, and then discuss the book with a parent or mentor.

The Second Step

Once you've done this with a classic, including reading it, taking handwritten notes as you read, participating in a group discussion of the book, and then talking with your parent or mentor about what could have made the discussion even better, then you are ready for Step 2.

Here it is: read a second great book and take lots of handwritten notes, and make a plan to improve the discussion experience this time (based on what you liked and disliked about the first discussion). Get your parent's or teacher's help. Then implement the plan. Participate in a discussion. Have fun with it.

The Third Step

Repeat this. Over and over. Do it at least once a month during your Practice Year, or do it every two weeks, or even weekly, if you like. If the Discussion Method is new to you, it may help to purposefully have several book discussions that include a parent or mentor (or someone else experienced in the Discussion Method) who can help take the discussion beyond the level of "Did you like the book?" Alternatively, listening to a few book discussions from the Mentoring in the Classics series or the TJEd High! Mentoring videos could be a valuable aid in increasing the quality of the discussions.

At some point you'll want to do this a lot, to almost make it your full-time educational focus, by filling your days with great books, great discussions, great learning. But until you do, just play around with it. Do it for fun. A little at a time. Do math, science, and other topics that interest you at the same time.

Do more when you feel like it. Do less when you'd prefer.

Enjoy!

Relax. Someday soon you'll launch yourself way more into it. You'll read and discuss intensely, deeply, for hours and hours and hours. If you're ready right now, go for it. If not, just practice it a bit.

No rush. You'll get there.

Especially for Parents

Note to parents: Relax. The time will come when your youth will be so focused on great reading and discussions that it will be hard to find the time to get him/her to do chores or sit down to just talk with you. It will be all great classics all the time. So for now, enjoy that he/she has more time to just talk to you, and have fun. Enjoy this while it lasts.

No rush.

He'll get there. She'll get there.

While you're waiting, read more great books yourself. This way, when your teens get there, you'll be even better prepared as a mentor. It's more than okay if they take their time. That gives you time to read more classics. Have fun with it. Let them wash the dishes while you read and discuss great ideas. Seriously. Let them do more chores, while you do more reading. The tables will be reversed soon enough. For now, enjoy.

During the course of this year, have your youth and you periodically read things that help him or her gain the vision and mindset of Scholar Phase, like:

- *Thomas Jefferson Education for Teens*

- Chapters 6 - 7 of *The Phases of Learning*

- "Youth Versus Teenager" by Michael Platt (on the TJEd website)

Also, have your youth re-read chapters 1-2 of this book every 90 days or so. There is power in having the *expectation* of a real Scholar Phase. When parents and youth are clear on what it means and why it matters, the transition becomes natural, also making it natural for parents to take a more patient and optimistic approach to the Practice Year. It's important for you to re-read the same chapters as well.

Seriously: Every 90 days or less, re-read chapters 1 and 2. You'll learn more each time through. This is your template for great learning. Go back to it frequently.

And, at the same time, enjoy reading and discussing various great books. This is what the Practice Year is all about. Do it well, and you'll soon be excited to launch into the first Intense Reading Year.

5

Year One

"One of the most fundamental and important techniques of great leadership reading is a fantastic technology known as the pen. It is amazing what this one little device (assuming you actually use it) can do for a reader's learning and success. In fact, using it just once through a book can have a lasting impact on generations of potential leaders—anyone who comes along later and reads the marked-up book. That's right! Write in your books. All of them."

–TURN THE PAGE

*"Success consists of going from failure to failure
without a loss of enthusiasm."*

–ATTRIBUTED TO WINSTON CHURCHILL

THIS quote, often attributed to Winston Churchill, came into my life at exactly the right time. I was in the midst of a major writer's block. The book I was working on was important, and I had a looming deadline, yet I just couldn't seem to get into it. I would sit down to write, only to stare at the screen, then put it away and go find something else to do. This happened over and over.

Finally, I decided to take a break from trying to write for a couple of days. Even though the deadline was getting closer, I knew I had to change things up or I wouldn't make any progress. Then the couple of days turned into a couple of weeks, and I was no closer to finishing the book. I was stressed, and overwhelmed.

One late night (actually, it was around 4 in the morning), I decided that enough is enough. I just had to get back to writing, and the writing needed to be high quality. I pulled out a blank piece of paper and began brainstorming ways to get past my writer's block.

I jotted down a number of ideas, from starting on a different book or just quitting to taking a vacation or calling the publisher and pushing back the deadline. During this process I began listing immediate actions I could take that might jolt me back into writing mode, things like "go buy a big chocolate shake and let the sugar knock some sense into my brain," "go camping today—maybe the pines, aspens, deer and elk will help me feel more inspired," and "drive to Walmart right now."

The last item on the list seemed pretty dumb. Drive to Walmart? Really? What good would that do?

It was 4 a.m., very dark outside, and Walmart was one of the few places in my small town that was open 24 hours a day. It was the one thing on the list I could do immediately. I read through the list, checking each item against my gut feelings.

Camping	Didn't feel right
Quitting	Not a good idea
Postponing	Bad
Chocolate Shake	Uh…tempting—but no (like that'll help!)
Walmart	Somehow it just felt…*right*

I got in the car and drove. Once at Walmart, I decided the whole thing was a pretty silly idea. How was I going to get past writer's block just from walking around looking at stuff?

But I did it anyway, and I soon found myself in the book section skimming books that looked interesting. Somewhere along the way I hit pay dirt.

I came across the following quote by Winston Churchill:

> "Success consists of going from failure to failure
> without a loss of enthusiasm."

I read it, then read it again. I was stunned. "That's it!" I said aloud. I looked around to see if anyone heard me talking to myself. At 4:40 a.m. there was nobody in sight.

I read the quote once more.

I shook my head. "It's not writer's block that's the problem," I told myself. "It's that I've allowed writer's block to take away my enthusiasm. I need to get excited and happy, regardless of whether I have writer's block or not."

I don't remember the rest of the story. Clearly I started writing again at some point, because I finished the book on time. But I don't recall what else happened. It just wasn't all that important.

Instead, I remember what really worked. I went home and brainstormed things I love to do, things to get excited about, and I put my energy into them. This changed everything. When I was enthusiastic, engaged, and happy, the writing took care of itself.

Keep Reading

Success really is about going from failure to failure without losing your enthusiasm. When you stay enthused, the hard things in life (and we all have them) take a back seat to the positive things. They just do. When a project or process is tough, we have to keep our enthusiasm high.

This is the key to success in the first Intense Reading Year of Scholar Phase. What does this year look like? Lots of reading. Lots of discussion. More reading. More discussion.

It's all about hours and days and weeks and months of reading. Reading and taking notes in great classics from many fields of knowledge. Fun novels. Intriguing commentaries. Leadership, self-improvement, and self-help books. Science books, math books, and art books. Skinny books and fat books. Short books and long books. Books with large type and books with small type. Lots and lots of words.

All followed with discussion. Discussion with a friend when you finish reading a great book, and sometimes with a group of friends. Discussion with a parent, or both parents, or your friends and their parents. Discussions with a teacher or other mentors. And always—always!—discussion with self in the form of handwritten notes in the margins and end-pages of books you are reading.

In short, this is a year of reading. What do you read? Things you want to read, and things you and your parents think would be good to read. Make a list of 10 books at a time, review the list with your parents and adjust, and read them. Then, as soon as you're done, meet again and make another list of 10. Keep doing it.

In the same meetings, plan discussion times and set them up.

Make it fun.

Read and Discuss
Read and Discuss
Read and Discuss

How much should you do it? As much as you like, plus just a tiny bit more. Push yourself, just a little. Don't push to the point that you burn out. Just to the point that you're loving it, plus it's hard work.

If you get tired, it's okay to stop. It's okay to go at the pace you like, but do push yourself some. And keep reading and discussing.

For a year.

Many Months

This should fill a *school* year, actually, which in many public schools lasts about 9 months but for homeschoolers is often about 10 months. Wherever you learn, try to get at least 10 months of reading (along with taking lots of handwritten notes) and discussing. Pick good classics as well as just really fun books. Take notes on all of them, and discuss as many of them as you can.

Then, after 10 months of this, take a 2-month summer break before going on to the next year. By the way, the summer break doesn't actually have to occur during the months of June, July, or August. Take the break when it fits your schedule. Again, plan the details with your parent(s). Alternatively, some people prefer to read steadily for about 6 weeks, then take a week or two off. If you follow this plan year round, you'll get your "summer" break in smaller doses.

As you're doing this all year, you'll sometimes do really well. At other times, however, you'll probably fall a bit short. You'll fail to read as much as you planned, or you'll dislike certain books and find yourself avoiding them even though you had planned to read them.

That's okay. Really.

But it's only okay as long as you keep your enthusiasm for reading and discussing. You can fall short on anything else, but don't lose your enthusiasm.

Remember Churchill's wisdom: "Success consists of going from failure to failure without a loss of enthusiasm." If you get tired, overwhelmed, or don't want to read something, that's okay. Don't read it. But stay enthusiastic and read something else instead.

In fact, to make this easier and more fun, when you plan your 10 books with your parent or other mentor, plan out two backup books as well. Then, if one of the 10 books bogs you down, set it aside and read the other nine. When you're done, read one of the backup books. Or try going back to the book you didn't like and see if it clicks with you now. If not, you have backups!

If you run out of backups, it's time for a meeting with your mentor to plan another 10 books (and two new backups). Keep doing this.

Communication Matters

Note that almost everyone struggles a little bit with this during the first year. After all, it's filled with so much reading, and building that habit can take time and perseverance. If you find yourself struggling, push yourself. Or, if you prefer, take a week off. Then come back to your books and start reading again. Do this whenever you need to. But communicate about your studies with your parent/mentor. Keep them in the loop, whatever you're doing. For example:

- "I'm reading *Tom Sawyer* this week. When I finish, I'm planning to read either *Huckleberry Finn* or *The Phantom Tollbooth* next."

- "I'm really struggling with *Little Women*, so I think
  I'm going to set it aside and move on to the next
  book on my list, which is *The Chosen*."

- "I want to read one of my backups, *Pride and Prejudice,*
  instead of *The Jungle Book*. I'm not sure why, but *The
  Jungle Book* just isn't clicking for me right now."

- "I want to take a day or two off from reading. Is that
  okay? I'm really tired. I just need to take a little break and
  get my love of reading back. What do you think?"

If you keep your parents/mentors up to date and informed, they can help you stay on task. Sometimes they'll help you talk through what's holding you back and fix it. Other times they'll just happily agree that you should skip a book or take a break. But talk over the details as you go.

It's also okay to push yourself to do things that seem boggy, but that feel important to you. After all, part of getting a Scholar Phase is learning to dig into the things that you don't necessarily want to learn, but desperately want to *know*. You are getting closer and closer to adulthood, and you can do hard things. You are up to this.

That said, there will be time in the later years of Scholar Phase to focus on the really tough things, so you don't have to go out of your way to push yourself at this stage of the game. Feel it out and do what seems right. Communicate with those who are helping and guiding you through the process, and always, always keep your enthusiasm.

To Parents (and other Mentors)

If your Scholar Phase student wants to set a book aside, skip it, or replace it with a backup, it's worth asking why. Don't be judgmental, just helpful. You want this reading year to be consistent, but not too demanding.

And sometimes you'll want to read the book she is skipping yourself to see if you can help her get past whatever's keeping her from loving it. Maybe you'll decide it's a good book to skip as well. Or perhaps you'll love it and be able to discuss why you love it with your Scholar Phase youth.

In general, let the student make the final decision, but communicate about it, and discuss options and reasons for her choices. Be supportive. Help her wisely overcome challenges when needed, or give herself a break and encourage her not to beat herself up when she really should just skip a certain book or take a break for a few days. This isn't about getting through a certain book. It's about gaining an appetite for serious study. Shutting her down in Reading Year 1 is not a great plan. In fact, be really careful not to push the Reading Year before the youth is ready to leave Practice level. This is a common mistake, and an excellent way to diminish your budding scholar's initiative and derail the Scholar Phase progress.

The purpose of this first Intense Reading Year is to do a lot of reading, note-taking, and discussing, while still staying in love with learning. Take it slow, and sometimes fast (when it's fun), and keep doing it. Reading and discussing—over and over and over.

A key role for parents/mentors during this year is to help plan, organize, and facilitate discussions. Your student doesn't need to discuss every book she reads in some big event, but she should have at least one event-based discussion a month (online or in person), and at least one smaller family-oriented discussion a month. As the year progresses, she will likely benefit from even more discussions.

Some of these discussions can be arranged online, as long as you are careful about her online connections. For example, TJEd High! has a dedicated online discussion environment that doesn't have newsfeeds or random interlopers. Wherever your youth discuss, be mindful of Internet safety and be sure they are aware of your rules for privacy and protection.

In both local and online discussion, either participate yourself or be sure other adults that you trust are present and involved. And where possible, read the books she is reading for event discussions and either attend and participate yourself, or supplement the event with further discussion between you and your student (preferably before an event discussion). Read your own copy of the book, and mark it up with your own handwritten notes.

You don't have to read every book your scholar does, but try to ask her about each book she finishes and have her share her main ideas and thoughts about it with you. These discussions will significantly increase the quality of her learning—and you'll be able to clearly see if, and how, she's progressing.

Sample Reading Lists

Below we've provided a number of sample reading lists, but they are only samples, not curriculum. It's best during the Intense Reading Years to drop any pre-structured curriculum and personalize the reading plan to the needs of each individual student. These samples certainly aren't meant to be required lists.

Use them to consider what to read when you are making your lists of 10 books and two backups. Choose the ones that seem most interesting to you, and make the list with guidance and input from your parent(s) and/ or mentor. Don't worry too much over this. You don't have to select the "perfect" list every time. You'll have time to read them all eventually, and others as well. The purpose of these sample lists is just to get you started.

If you have already read some of the books on this list, consider reading them again with your newfound skills of writing in the margins and holding discussions of varying types about each book. Not only are great books worth reading over and over—it's the fourth and fifth time through that brings the most value, in my experience. Really! So if you are in a position to re-read and be in a discussion of a book you've already covered, don't shy away; consider it a golden opportunity! Also, it's good to mix books that seem fun with books you feel you really ought to read. The sample lists below reflect this kind of mixture.

If you want to get more of a sense of what a certain book is about before you put it on your list, try looking it up on Amazon and reading the summary or, where available, previewing what's inside the book itself. Or, better still, if you already have a copy or can find one in your local library, just glance at the table of contents and randomly open the book and read a few paragraphs. This kind of preview actually helps your mind process the book beforehand so you'll learn more when you read it.

Another help is to mix story-based books with other titles that are more essay-based. Both fiction and non-fiction are valuable. Again, the sample lists provide examples of such combinations.

Some of the books on sample lists or other great book lists you find will likely seem interesting right off the bat—start with those. And some books may seem like something you really don't want to read. You can put those aside for now, but at some point do pick the books that just don't resonate with you—they frequently turn out to be some of the best things you'll read.

Also, try to include some books that your parent or mentor has already read. This will allow her to read through it again—and she'll have even deeper insight to share with you. If you're going to discuss a certain book with a group, consider letting members of the group take part in choosing which book(s) to read. But don't have the group determine your entire list of 10. Do most of the choosing yourself, and with your parent/mentor. Or, if you are in a TJEd-style class, get excited about the assigned books, and also read others that interest you.

If you don't know where to start, you can begin by finding out which of the books on the sample lists below (or others like them) are already available in your home. If you already have them, that's a good place to begin. Get your parent's permission before you write in their books—same if you're using a sibling's book. If they don't want you to write in it, try to get your own copy if possible.

You can also go to your local library and see which books they have ready to go. This makes things easy. However, when you read library books you won't write in the margins, so you'll have to find another way to take notes. Again, it's best to get and read your own copy of the book whenever possible—so you can write in it and keep your notes in case you re-read it later. If this isn't possible, keep notes in other ways, such as a notebook or binder dedicated to your handwritten notes on books, and make it as permanent a feature in your life as possible, so you can keep those powerful ideas and pieces of your education for future re-reads and discussions. You can even transfer your notes into the books as you eventually get your own copy of each.

Another option in choosing what to read is to simply pick one of the following sample lists and read the books it recommends. Some people find this approach simple and rewarding. But it's okay to pick and choose and make your own lists if you prefer. Once you have your list of 10, read them in any order. You're going to read them all anyway, so just pick one and dig in.

Some people like to read one book at a time, while others prefer to read several books simultaneously. In Scholar Phase, reading several books at once is the best approach for most people, because if you get tired of one book you can just put it down and keep reading something else. It's no different than having a plate full of dinner with several things to eat, and picking some of this, then some of that. It keeps your mind active, fresh and curious when you switch things up that way.

Of course, if you become deeply enthralled in a certain book you'll likely want to read it all the way through, because it's hard to put it down when you're so engaged. That's fine—great, even. One of the best parts of this stage of Scholar Phase is being able to dig into all sorts of books, finding some of the ones that'll stick with you throughout life, and also enjoying the ones that are just plain fun. In short: Try to have several books going at once, but feel free to keep reading one if you're excited about it and don't want to quit.

You're going to be reading a lot, so don't wait for your friends, parent, or mentor to discuss each book with you before you start reading the next book. It's okay to share the lessons you've learned from a book even if the other person hasn't read it yet. Just use your notes, and tell them the most important things you learned. At times, you'll read small or even large piles of books before you get around to discussing any of them with other people. But you'll have your own handwritten discussions in the margins.

Time to Choose

Before we get to the sample lists, here are a few books that pretty much everyone should read right away. I recommend that you include them as part of your first 10 books. They will help you learn more effectively and make this first Intense Reading Year even more fun.

- The First 3!
  - *Turn the Page* (Brady)
  - *Thomas Jefferson Education for Teens* (DeMille and Brooks)
  - *The Five Love Languages of Teenagers* (Chapman)

You'll get the most from these if you discuss them with others after you've read each one. Also, if there are any books from the list in the Practice Year chapter that you haven't read yet, try to include them in your reading as soon as possible. All of them are great reading, and they each contain very important principles and ideas. You probably read some of them last year, but if not, consider reading them soon.

Above all, have fun. Push yourself a little, but have fun while you're doing it.

Take some time to read through each of the sample lists below and really think about them. Circle books that seem interesting to you, and others that you're sure you want to read soon. Mark some that you know you want to read later, at some point. Come to really know these lists. Think about each title, and put together your own list of 10 books and 2 backups to begin your Intense Reading.

Again, have fun with this!

List of 10 — Sample A	List of 10 — Sample B
The Five Love Languages of Teenagers (Chapman)	*The Five Love Languages of Teenagers* (Chapman)
Thomas Jefferson Education for Teens (DeMille and Brooks)	*Thomas Jefferson Education for Teens* (DeMille and Brooks)
Turn the Page (Brady)	*Turn the Page* (Brady)
The Phantom Tollbooth (Juster)	*The Great Brain* (Fitzgerald)
*Carry On Mr. Bowditch (Latham)	**The Cricket in Times Square* (Seldon and Williams)
Trumpet of the Swan (White)	*Pawn of Prophecy* (Eddings)
Little Women (Alcott)	*Little Men* (Alcott)
Anne of Green Gables (Montgomery)	Book on mathematics (whatever level you are at)
We Hold These Truths to Be Self-Evident (DeMille)	*Tom Sawyer* (Twain)
*Prince Caspian (Lewis)	*"Give Me Liberty or Give Me Death" (Henry)
Backups	**Backups**
Do Hard Things (Harris and Harris)	*The Inner Ring* (Lewis)
The Declaration of Independence	*Anne of Green Gables* (Montgomery)

(Note: the * symbol on these lists mark each fifth book on a list.)

List of 10 — Sample C	List of 10 — Sample D
The Five Love Languages of Teenagers (Chapman)	*The Five Love Languages of Teenagers* (Chapman)
Thomas Jefferson Education for Teens (DeMille and Brooks)	*Thomas Jefferson Education for Teens* (DeMille and Brooks)
Turn the Page (Brady)	*Turn the Page* (Brady)
The Jungle Book (Kipling)	*A Midsummer's Night Dream* (Shakespeare)
The Rithmatist (Sanderson)	*Mistborn* (Sanderson)
Book on mathematics (whatever level you are at)	*A Beginner's Guide to Constructing the Universe* (Schneider)
The Real Thomas Jefferson (Allison)	*A Thomas Jefferson Education* (DeMille)
Dumbing Us Down (Gatto)	*Here There Be Dragons* (Owen)
The Chosen (Potok)	*Archimedes and the Door of Science* (Bendick)
Little Britches (Moody)	*Spiritual Lives of the Great Composers* (Kavanaugh)
Backups	**Backups**
Jane Eyre (Bronte)	*Jo's Boys* (Alcott)
The Lonesome Gods (L'Amour)	*Romeo and Juliet* (Shakespeare)

List of 10 — Sample E	List of 10 — Sample F
The Five Love Languages of Teenagers (Chapman)	*The Five Love Languages of Teenagers* (Chapman)
Thomas Jefferson Education for Teens (DeMille and Brooks)	*Thomas Jefferson Education for Teens* (DeMille and Brooks)
Turn the Page (Brady)	*Turn the Page* (Brady)
All's Well That Ends Well (Shakespeare)	*The Lion, the Witch, and the Wardrobe* (Lewis)
Math Doesn't Suck (McKellar)	*Little House in the Big Woods* (Wilder)
The 7 Habits of Highly Effective Teens (Covey)	*Pollyanna* (Porter)
Best Loved Poems of the American People (Felleman and Allen)	*On Numbers* (Asimov)
Sonnets (Shakespeare)	Book on mathematics (whatever level you are at)
Rascal (Brady)	*LeaderShift* (Woodward and DeMille)
Bendigo Shafter (L'Amour)	*"I Have a Dream"* (King)
Backups	**Backups**
The Mallorean (Eddings)	*The Mistborn Trilogy* (Sanderson)
Julius Caesar (Shakespeare)	*A Tale of Two Cities* (Dickens)

List of 10 — Sample G	List of 10 — Sample H
The Five Love Languages of Teenagers (Chapman)	*The Five Love Languages of Teenagers* (Chapman)
Thomas Jefferson Education for Teens (DeMille and Brooks)	*Thomas Jefferson Education for Teens* (DeMille and Brooks)
Turn the Page (Brady)	*Turn the Page* (Brady)
The Tempest (Shakespeare)	*Elantris* (Sanderson)
*Introduction to Mathematics (Whitehead)	**Mythology* (Hamilton)
Aesop's Fables	*Saint Joan* (Twain)
Huckleberry Finn (Twain)	*The Law* (Bastiat)
Resolved (Woodward)	*The Jackrabbit Factor* (Householder)
The Science of Getting Rich (Wattles)	*Say*Go*Be*Do* (Earl)
*Pride and Prejudice (Austen)	**The Walking Drum* (L'Amour)
Backups	**Backups**
1913 (DeMille)	*Sense and Sensibility* (Austen)
Hamlet (Shakespeare)	*Animal Farm* (Orwell)

Keep On Reading!

Of course, there are a lot of other books to choose from. A book doesn't have to be on some special list to teach you a lot. In fact, by this point you know that it's the *way* you read, take notes and engage discussions that largely determine how greatly you learn.

Remember: It's okay to fall short as you make plans and try to implement them, but always keep your enthusiasm up! If one book doesn't work, read another. And just keep reading. It's kind of like the *Finding Nemo* or *Finding Dory* approach to learning:

Just keep reading!

Just keep reading!

Just keep reading, reading, reading!

What do we do? We Read!!

And throw in a lot of discussion as well.

Now, put together your first list of 10 books and 2 backups and get started!

6
Year Two

*"There is hardly a pioneer's hut that does not contain a few
odd volumes of Shakespeare. I remember that I read the feudal drama
of Henry V for the first time in a log cabin."*
—ALEXIS DE TOCQUEVILLE, DEMOCRACY IN AMERICA

*"The goal in all this is not simply to get your children to read...
the point is to raise them to be truly in love with reading,
so it'll be something they do and use for the rest of their lives."*
—CHRIS BRADY

IN the Second Year of Intense Reading, it's time to get really serious. It's time to bring in true intensity. It's time to read for hours and hours, week after week, month after month. This is where Scholar Phase really kicks into full swing.

The purpose of this year is to read. A lot. And then read even more. This can be a very fun year, if the student truly gets into it and focuses on reading and discussing. It is not necessary to discuss every book with other people, but by taking good notes a lot of internal discussion occurs. The more the better.

This is a year for the pursuit of knowledge, wisdom, and deeper understanding. It is a time to fall in love with study, and with ideas. At its best, this is a period of enthusiastically reading with abandon and focus—book after book after book.

It is important during this year to read things that interest you, and also a few things that are worth reading even if they don't interest you as much.

Read several books simultaneously, so if you lose interest in one after an hour or a few hours you can go right on to reading something else. And read books from around the curriculum, meaning from many topics and fields of knowledge.

Have fun, and push yourself. Push yourself much more than in the past. This year is when Scholar Phase and your education really flourish—where the rubber hits the road, where you walk the talk. This is the year to make it happen. All excuses aside: read, read, read. And discuss as you go.

The Big List

Following is the great Scholar Phase reading list. Read other things beyond this list—anything you find interesting and valuable. And try to read everything on this list as well.

Check off what you read as you go. But don't just read and check things off the list in a rote manner. Go slow enough to take good margin notes, or notes in a dedicated notebook or binder for books that you don't own. Have important discussions with the author and yourself as you read each book. Go deep. Think broadly. And keep reading!

Take some time to study this list for a few minutes. Mark any that you have already read, and note any that excite you right now. Use this list to make a plan for the coming week, and get started on several books!

Definite Reads

10

- [ ] *The Five Love Languages of Teenagers* (Chapman)
- [ ] *Thomas Jefferson Education for Teens* (DeMille and Brooks)
- [ ] *Turn the Page* (Brady)
- [ ] *The Phantom Tollbooth* (Juster)
- [ ] *Carry On, Mr. Bowditch* (Latham)
- [ ] *Trumpet of the Swan* (White)
- [ ] *Little Women* (Alcott)
- [ ] *Anne of Green Gables* (Montgomery)
- [ ] *We Hold These Truths to Be Self-Evident* (DeMille)
- [ ] "Give Me Liberty or Give Me Death" (Henry)

20

- ☐ *Do Hard Things* (Harris and Harris)
- ☐ *The Great Brain* (Fitzgerald)
- ☐ *The Cricket in Times Square* (Seldon and Williams)
- ☐ *Pawn of Prophecy*, book 1 of *The Belgariad* (Eddings)
- ☐ *Little Men* (Alcott)
- ☐ *Tom Sawyer* (Twain)
- ☐ *The Rithmatist* (Sanderson)
- ☐ *The Law* (Bastiat)
- ☐ *The 5,000 Year Leap* (Skousen)
- ☐ *The Declaration of Independence*

30

- ☐ *Queen of Sorcery*, book 2 of *The Belgariad* (Eddings)
- ☐ *Magician's Gambit*, book 3 of *The Belgariad* (Eddings)
- ☐ *Castle of Wizardry*, book 4 of *The Belgariad* (Eddings)
- ☐ *Enchanter's End Game*, book 5 of *The Belgariad* (Eddings)
- ☐ "The Inner Ring" (Lewis)
- ☐ *The Jungle Book* (Kipling)
- ☐ *Dumbing Us Down* (Gatto)
- ☐ *Little Britches* (Moody)
- ☐ *The Chosen* (Potok)
- ☐ *The Real Thomas Jefferson* (Allison)

40

- ☐ *The Lonesome Gods* (L'Amour)
- ☐ *Archimedes and the Door of Science* (Bendick)
- ☐ *Jo's Boys* (Alcott)
- ☐ *A Midsummer's Night Dream* (Shakespeare)
- ☐ *Mistborn* book 1 of trilogy (Sanderson)
- ☐ *The Well of Ascension*, book 2 of *Mistborn* trilogy (Sanderson)
- ☐ *The Hero of Ages*, book 3 of *Mistborn* trilogy, (Sanderson)
- ☐ *Math Doesn't Suck* (McKellar)
- ☐ *Spiritual Lives of the Great Composers* (Kavanaugh)
- ☐ *Jane Eyre* (Bronte)

50

- ☐ *Here There Be Dragons* (Owen)
- ☐ *A Thomas Jefferson Education* (DeMille)

☐ *A Beginner's Guide to Constructing the Universe* (Schneider)
☐ *Guardians of the West*, book 1 of *The Mallorean* (Eddings)
☐ *King of the Murgos*, book 2 of *The Mallorean* (Eddings)
☐ *Demon Lord of Karanda*, book 3 of *The Mallorean* (Eddings)
☐ *Sorceress of Darshiva*, book 4 of *The Mallorean* (Eddings)
☐ *The Seeress of Kell*, book 5 of *The Mallorean* (Eddings)
☐ *All's Well That Ends Well* (Shakespeare)
☐ *Kiss My Math* (McKellar)

60

☐ *The 7 Habits of Highly Effective Teens* (Covey)
☐ *Best Loved Poems of the American People* (Felleman and Allen)
☐ *Sonnets* (Shakespeare)
☐ *Rascal* (Brady)
☐ *Bendigo Shafter* (L'Amour)
☐ *Julius Caesar* (Shakespeare)
☐ *The Lion, the Witch, and the Wardrobe* (Lewis)
☐ *Little House in the Big Woods* (Wilder)
☐ *Pollyanna* (Porter)
☐ *LeaderShift* (Woodward and DeMille)

70

☐ *"I Have a Dream"* (King)
☐ *On Numbers* (Asimov)
☐ *A Tale of Two Cities* (Dickens)
☐ *Huckleberry Finn* (Twain)
☐ *Aesop's Fables*
☐ *The Tempest* (Shakespeare)
☐ *Introduction to Mathematics* (Whitehead)
☐ *Resolved* (Woodward)
☐ *Pride and Prejudice* (Austen)
☐ *The Science of Getting Rich* (Wattles)

80

☐ *Mythology* (Hamilton)
☐ *Elantris* (Sanderson)
☐ *Saint Joan* (Twain)
☐ *The Walking Drum* (L'Amour)
☐ *The Jackrabbit Factory* (Householder)

☐ *Say*Go*Be*Do* (Earl)
☐ *Animal Farm* (Orwell)
☐ *Sense and Sensibility* (Austen)
☐ *1913* (DeMille)
☐ *Hamlet* (Shakespeare)

90

☐ *Alice in Wonderland* (Carroll)
☐ *Financial Fitness for Teens* (Brady)
☐ *Ender's Game* (Card)
☐ *The Wizard of Oz* (Baum)
☐ *Anthem* (Rand)
☐ *Little House on the Prairie* (Wilder)
☐ *Flatland* (Abbott)
☐ *The Real Benjamin Franklin* (Allison)
☐ *The Fourth Turning* (Strauss and Howe)
☐ *The Constitution of the United States*

100

☐ *The Making of America* (Skousen)
☐ *The Cashflow Quadrant* (Kiyosaki)
☐ *The One Minute Manager* (Blanchard and Johnson)
☐ *A Whole New Mind* (Pink)
☐ *Leadership Education: The Phases of Learning* (DeMille and DeMille)
☐ *The Hiding Place* (Boom)
☐ *Oedipus Rex* (Sophocles)
☐ *Antigone* (Sophocles)
☐ *The Real George Washington* (Parry)
☐ *The Monroe Doctrine*

110

☐ "The Gettysburg Address" (Lincoln)
☐ *The Deerslayer* (Cooper)
☐ *Iliad* (Homer)
☐ *First Things First* (Covey)
☐ *As a Man Thinketh* (Allen)
☐ *Odyssey* (Homer)
☐ *The Trial and Death of Socrates* in four dialogues (Plato)
☐ *Emma* (Austen)

☐ *Elements,* book I (Euclid)
☐ *Elements,* book II (Euclid)

120
☐ *Elements,* book III (Euclid)
☐ *A Connecticut Yankee in King Arthur's Court* (Twain)
☐ *Les Miserables* (Hugo)
☐ *Democracy in America,* volume I (Tocqueville)
☐ *Democracy in America,* volume II (Tocqueville)
☐ *Notebooks* (DaVinci)
☐ *Narrative of the Life of Frederick Douglass* (Douglass)
☐ *The Hunchback of Notre Dame* (Hugo)
☐ *Arithmetic* (Nichomachus)
☐ *Wild at Heart* (Eldridge)

130
☐ *Othello* (Shakespeare)
☐ *Captivating* (Eldridge)
☐ *The Coming Aristocracy* (DeMille)
☐ *The Art of War* (Tzu)
☐ *In Flanders Field* (McCrae)
☐ *The Eighth Habit* (Covey)
☐ *Freedom Matters* (DeMille)
☐ *The Alchemist* (Coelho)
☐ *Poetry and Mathematics* (Buchanan)
☐ *The Fellowship of the Ring* (Tolkien)

140
☐ *The Two Towers* (Tolkien)
☐ *The Return of the King* (Tolkien)
☐ *Foundation,* book 1 (Asimov)
☐ *Foundation and Empire,* book 2 of *Foundation* trilogy (Asimov)
☐ *Second Foundation,* book 3 of *Foundation* trilogy (Asimov)
☐ *The Student Whisperer* (DeMille and Earl)
☐ *Where the Red Fern Grows* (Rawls)
☐ *Man of the Family* (Moody)
☐ *A Brief History of Time* (Hawking)
☐ "The Present Crisis" (Lowell)

150

- ☐ *The Republic* (Plato)
- ☐ *Politics* (Aristotle)
- ☐ *The U.S. Constitution and the 196 Indispensible Principles of Freedom* (DeMille)
- ☐ *Relativity* (Einstein)
- ☐ *"What is Seen, What is Not Seen"* (Bastiat) .
- ☐ *"The Proper Role of Government"* (Benson)
- ☐ *The Tao of Physics* (Capra)
- ☐ *Orthodoxy* (Chesterton)
- ☐ *Analects* (Confucius)
- ☐ *On the Revolutions of the Heavenly Spheres* (Copernicus)

160

- ☐ *Laddie* (Stratton-Porter)
- ☐ *Alas Babylon* (Frank)
- ☐ The Dred Scott Decision (Supreme Court Case)
- ☐ *The Closing of the American Mind* (Bloom)
- ☐ *The Tools of Money* (Life Leadership)
- ☐ *Financial Fitness* (Brady and Woodward)
- ☐ *Mentoring Matters* (Woodward)
- ☐ *FreedomShift* (DeMille)
- ☐ *The Abolition of Man* (Lewis)
- ☐ *The Federalist Papers* (Madison)

170

- ☐ *Aeneid* (Virgil)
- ☐ *SPLASH!: A Leader's Guide to Effective Public Speaking* (Brady)
- ☐ *The Happiness Equation* (Pasricha)
- ☐ *Georgics* (Virgil)
- ☐ *Passion-Driven Education* (Boyack)
- ☐ *Give Your Child the World* (Jamie Martin)
- ☐ *As You Like It* (Shakespeare)
- ☐ *Uncommon Sense* (Palmer)
- ☐ *Charlotte's Web* (White)
- ☐ *The Promise* (Potok)

180

- ☐ *The History of Freedom* (Acton)

☐ *The Arabian Knights* (Burton)
☐ *Brighty of the Grand Canyon* (Henry and Dennis)
☐ *Understood Betsy* (Fisher)
☐ *The Other Greeks* (Hanson)
☐ *A Christmas Carol* (Dickens)
☐ *Seventh Letter* (Plato)
☐ *Divergent* (Roth)
☐ "The Road Not Taken" (Frost)
☐ "The Man With the Hoe" (Markham)

190

☐ "Self-Reliance" (Emerson)
☐ *A Man for All Seasons* (Bolt)
☐ *Persuasion* (Austen)
☐ *Henry V* (Shakespeare)
☐ *The Autobiography of Benjamin Franklin*
☐ *Hot X!: Algebra Exposed* (McKellar)
☐ *The Winter's Tale* (Shakespeare)
☐ *King Lear* (Shakespeare)
☐ *12 Years a Slave* (Northup)
☐ *Pericles* (Shakespeare)

200

(The Next 10 Books are Extremely
Challenging — Work Closely With a Mentor)
☐ *Romeo and Juliet* (Shakespeare)
☐ *Macbeth* (Shakespeare)
☐ *Lord of the Flies* (Goulding)
☐ *1984* (Orwell)
☐ *The Hunger Games* (Collins)
☐ *Catching Fire* (Collins)
☐ *Mockingjay* (Collins)
☐ *My Name is Asher Lev* (Potok)
☐ *Brave New World* (Huxley)
☐ *The Giver* (Lowry)

Optional Reads

210

- ☐ *Prince Caspian* (Lewis)
- ☐ *The Hobbit* (Tolkien)
- ☐ *Nichomachaean Ethics* (Aristotle)
- ☐ *Measure for Measure* (Shakespeare)
- ☐ "Thoughts on Government" (Adams)
- ☐ *Meditations* (Aurelius)
- ☐ *The City of God* (Augustine)
- ☐ *The Power of Four* (Marshall)
- ☐ *Wuthering Heights* (Bronte)
- ☐ *The American Tradition* (Carson)

220

- ☐ "On Kingship" (Aquinas)
- ☐ *Laws* (Cicero)
- ☐ *On War* (Clausewitz)
- ☐ "An Invitation to the Pain of Learning" (Adler)
- ☐ *Call of the Wild* (London)
- ☐ *Republic* (Cicero)
- ☐ *White Fang* (London)
- ☐ *Dinotopia* (Gurney)
- ☐ *Robin Hood* (Pyle)
- ☐ *The Princess Bride* (Goldman)

230

- ☐ *Anne Frank: The Diary of a Young Girl*
- ☐ *Ben Hur* (Wallace)
- ☐ *The Princess Diaries* (Goldman)
- ☐ *Black Beauty* (Sewell)
- ☐ *The Black Stallion* (Farley)
- ☐ *The Collected Verse of Edgar A. Guest*
- ☐ *David Copperfield* (Dickens)
- ☐ *Don Quixote* (Cervantes)
- ☐ *Dr. Jekyll and Mr. Hyde* (Stevenson)
- ☐ *The Education of Henry Adams* (Adams)

240

- ☐ *Eight Cousins* (Alcott)

☐ *Frankenstein* (Shelley)
☐ *Gulliver's Travels* (Swift)
☐ *Heidi* (Spyri)
☐ *Ivanhoe* (Scott)
☐ *Island of the Blue Dolphins* (O'Dell)
☐ *The Last of the Mohicans* (Cooper)
☐ *Mathematicians Are People Too*, volume 1 (Reimer and Reimer)
☐ *Mathematicians Are People Too*, volume 2 (Reimer and Reimer)
☐ *The Count of Monte Cristo* (Dumas)

250
☐ *The Prince and the Pauper* (Twain)
☐ *National Velvet* (Bagnold)
☐ *Old Yeller* (Gipson and Armstrong)
☐ *Oliver Twist* (Dickens)
☐ *The Robe* (Douglas)
☐ *Robinson Crusoe* (DeFoe)
☐ *The Secret Garden* (Burnett)
☐ *Stuart Little* (White)
☐ *Summer of the Monkeys* (Rawls)
☐ *The Swiss Family Robinson* (Wyss)

260
☐ *The Comedy of Errors* (Shakespeare)
☐ *Sackett's Land* (L'Amour)
☐ *Jubal Sackett* (L'Amour)
☐ *Treasure Island* (Stevenson)
☐ *Twelfth Night* (Shakespeare)
☐ *The Many Speeches of Chief Seattle* (Gifford)
☐ *The Yearling* (Rawlings)
☐ "Ulysses" (Joyce)
☐ *The Land Was Everything* (Hanson)
☐ *The Voyages of Dr. Dolittle* (Lofting)

270
☐ *The Last of the Breed* (L'Amour)
☐ *The 7 Habits of Highly Effective People* (Covey)
☐ *The Divine Comedy* (Dante)
☐ *A Discourse on Method* (Descartes)

- ☐ *Magnificent Obsession* (Douglass)
- ☐ *Collected Essays of Ralph Waldo Emerson* (Emerson)
- ☐ *Two New Sciences* (Galileo)
- ☐ *History of Western Civilization*, volume 1 (Durant)
- ☐ *History of Western Civilization*, volume 2 (Durant)
- ☐ *History of Western Civilization*, volume 3 (Durant)

280

- ☐ *History of Western Civilization*, volume 4 (Durant)
- ☐ *History of Western Civilization*, volume 5 (Durant)
- ☐ *History of Western Civilization*, volume 6 (Durant)
- ☐ *History of Western Civilization*, volume 7 (Durant)
- ☐ *History of Western Civilization*, volume 8 (Durant)
- ☐ *History of Western Civilization*, volume 9 (Durant)
- ☐ *History of Western Civilization*, volume 10 (Durant)
- ☐ *History of Western Civilization*, volume 11 (Durant)
- ☐ *The Lessons of History* (Durant)
- ☐ *Civilization and It's Discontents* (Freud)

290

- ☐ *Faust* (Goethe)
- ☐ *Decline and Fall of the Roman Empire*, volume 1 (Gibbon)
- ☐ *Decline and Fall of the Roman Empire*, volume 2 (Gibbon)
- ☐ *Decline and Fall of the Roman Empire*, volume 3 (Gibbon)
- ☐ *Decline and Fall of the Roman Empire*, volume 4 (Gibbon)
- ☐ *Decline and Fall of the Roman Empire*, volume 5 (Gibbon)
- ☐ *Decline and Fall of the Roman Empire*, volume 6 (Gibbon)
- ☐ *Excellent Sheep* (Deresiewicz)
- ☐ *History of Warfare* (Keegan)
- ☐ *Epitome* (Kepler)

300

- ☐ *Leviathan* (Hobbes)
- ☐ *Essays Moral, Political, and Literary* (Hume)
- ☐ *Principia Mathematica* (Newton)
- ☐ *The Structure of Scientific Revolutions* (Kuhn)
- ☐ *Elements of Chemistry* (Lavoisier)
- ☐ *The Screwtape Letters* (Lewis)
- ☐ *The Weight of Glory* (Lewis)

- [ ] *Second Treatise of Government* (Locke)
- [ ] *The Prince* (Machiavelli)
- [ ] *Collected Speeches of Abraham Lincoln* (Lincoln)

310

- [ ] *The Communist Manifesto* (Marx and Engels)
- [ ] *Utopia* (More)
- [ ] *The Magna Charta*
- [ ] *On Liberty* (Mill)
- [ ] *Paradise Lost* (Milton)
- [ ] *Paradise Regained* (Milton)
- [ ] *The Spirit of the Laws* (Montesquieu)
- [ ] *Commentaries on the Laws of England*, Book 1 (Blackstone)
- [ ] *Lives* (Plutarch)
- [ ] *Histories* (Polybius)

320

- [ ] *The Northwest Ordinance*
- [ ] *Algamest* (Ptolemy)
- [ ] *To Kill a Mockingbird* (Lee)
- [ ] "A World Split Apart" (Solzhenitsyn)
- [ ] *Uncle Tom's Cabin* (Stowe)
- [ ] *Vanity Fair* (Thackeray)
- [ ] *Walden* (Thoreau)
- [ ] *History of the Peloponnesian War* (Thucydides)
- [ ] *Mainspring of Human Progress* (Weaver)
- [ ] *The Virginian* (Wister)

330

- [ ] *Great Expectations* (Dickens)
- [ ] *The Host* (Meyer)
- [ ] *War and Peace* (Tolstoy)
- [ ] *Reforming American Education* (Adler)
- [ ] *Teacher in America* (Barzun)
- [ ] *An Education for Our Time* (Bunting)
- [ ] *The Book of Virtues* (Bennett)
- [ ] *Multiple Intelligences* (Gardner)
- [ ] *Cultural Literacy* (Hirsch)
- [ ] *The Scarlet Pimpernel* (Orczy)

340

- [ ] *The Higher Learning in America* (Hutchins)
- [ ] *The Healing Power of Stories* (Taylor)
- [ ] *FutureShock* (Toffler)
- [ ] *Revolutionary Wealth* (Toffler)
- [ ] *Paradigm Shift* (Guzzardo)
- [ ] *The Three Musketeers* (Dumas)
- [ ] *The Third Wave* (Toffler)
- [ ] *The 5 S's of Money* (Laplanche)
- [ ] *Wild Swans* (Chang)
- [ ] *Bulfinch's Mythology*

350

- [ ] *The Oxbow Incident* (Clark)
- [ ] *The Old Man and the Sea* (Hemingway)
- [ ] *The Grapes of Wrath* (Steinbeck)
- [ ] *For Whom the Bell Tolls* (Hemingway)
- [ ] *Northanger Abbey* (Austen)
- [ ] *Of Mice and Men* (Steinbeck)
- [ ] *Seventh Letter* (Plato)
- [ ] *Confessions* (Augustine)
- [ ] *Drawing Out the Dragons* (Owen)
- [ ] *Troilus and Cressida* (Shakespeare)

360

- [ ] *Advancement of Learning* (Bacon)
- [ ] *King John* (Shakespeare)
- [ ] *On the Law of Nature and Nations* (Pufendorf)
- [ ] *The Rights of Man* (Paine)
- [ ] *Articles of Confederation*
- [ ] *View of the Constitution of the United States* (Tucker)
- [ ] *Pickwick Papers* (Dickens)
- [ ] *Economic Sophisms* (Bastiat)
- [ ] *Economic Harmonies* (Bastiat)
- [ ] *Rubaiyat* (Hayyam)

370

- [ ] *The American Commonwealth*, volume 1 (Bryce)
- [ ] *Gifts from the Sea* (Lindbergh)

☐ *America's Great Depression* (Rothbard)
☐ *The American Commonwealth,* volume 2 (Bryce)
☐ *The Catcher in the Rye* (Salinger)
☐ *Tartuffe* (Moliere)
☐ *The Would-Be Gentleman* (Moliere)
☐ *The Great Gatsby* (Fitzgerald)
☐ *The Red Badge of Courage* (Crane)
☐ *A Farewell to Arms* (Hemingway)

380

☐ *Twenty Thousand Leagues Under the Sea* (Verne)
☐ *Pilgrim's Progress* (Bunyan)
☐ *Candide* (Voltaire)
☐ *The Sea Wolf* (London)
☐ *The Canterbury Tales* (Chaucer)
☐ *Collected Poems* (Browning)
☐ *Collected Poems* (Dickinson)
☐ *The Adventures of Sherlock Holmes* (Doyle)
☐ *Taming of the Shrew* (Shakespeare)
☐ *Shane* (Schaefer)

390

☐ *The Time Machine* (Wells)
☐ *The History of Early Rome* (Livy)
☐ *The Talisman* (Scott)
☐ *Confessions* (Rousseau)
☐ *Middlemarch* (Eliot)
☐ *Siddhartha* (Hesse)
☐ *Emile* (Rousseau)
☐ *The Pearl* (Steinbeck)
☐ *The Pioneers* (Cooper)
☐ *Fahrenheit 451* (Bradbury)

400

(The Next 10 Books are Extremely Challenging—
Work Closely With a Mentor)
☐ *Human Action* (Mises)
☐ *The Wealth of Nations* (Smith)
☐ *Road to Serfdom* (Hayek)

☐ *Beyond Good and Evil* (Nietzsche)
☐ *The Naked Capitalist* (Skousen)
☐ *The Scarlet Letter* (Hawthorne)
☐ *Moby Dick* (Melville)
☐ *The Collected Works of William Shakespeare*
☐ *Atlas Shrugged* (Rand)
☐ *The Fountainhead* (Rand)

In addition to those listed, read the top religious books from your religion and leading books of the major world religions. Along with the math and science readings included on this list, study as much other math and science as you can.

Read as many of these books as you can this year—while going slowly enough to really learn. Start with the ones that interest you most, and check off each book on this list when you finish reading it. Add in other titles that interest you. There are a lot of great books that aren't on this list—find and read them as well. By the time you are done with Scholar Phase, you want to have read most of the books on this list (with some substitutions or additions for good measure).

Of course, as always, take good notes with each. Discuss at least two books per month with other people—in one-on-one or group discussions, in person, or online. And always: Read, read, read!

Note that just because a book is thicker or more challenging to read and study than another book, doesn't mean it's necessarily better. Some of the best books with the most important and deepest lessons are simple and/or short, like *Charlotte's Web*, *Henry V*, *Animal Farm*, or *The Chosen*. That said, the more challenging books have a lot of important lessons to teach as well.

In short, this is a year for as much reading as you can possibly muster. Have fun, read some more, and push yourself.

Your Scholar Phase is here!

7

Year Three

Weak	*Better*
He was not very often on time.	*He usually came late.*
He did not think that studying Latin was a sensible way to use one's time.	*He thought the study of Latin a waste of time.*
Did not remember	*Forgot*
He is a man who…	*He…*
Used for fuel purposes	*Used for fuel*
His story is a strange one.	*His story is strange.*
Trafalgar, which was Nelson's last battle,	*Trafalgar, Nelson's last battle…*

—*Elements of Style*

HE Third Intense Reading Year comes with a twist. Keep reading and reading, and then add in The Class as well.

The Class is very important. Here's how it works: During the Third Year of Intense Scholar Phase Reading, set up a Mom School (or a Dad School). This is a game-changer. It drastically increases the quality of each youth's learning and education.

The Power of a Mom School
(or a Dad School)

But what exactly does this mean? There are four major types of schools: conveyor belt schools (with a one-size-fits-all curriculum), professional schools (that train for a specific job or career), leadership schools (that prepare students by teaching them *how* to think and giving them other skills of great learning and life success), and Mom Schools. The first three are widely understood, but a Mom School is more rare. Put simply, a Mom School is created when a Mom (or other mentor) sees the need for a specific kind of class for her child—and sets it up, invites the right peers to join, and implements it for a few months or an entire school year.

A Mom School usually dissolves after it meets the needs of the child—since it has fulfilled its purpose and it is time for the child and parents to move on to different things. Mom Schools are often incredibly effective, because they are targeted at specific student needs at a given time and their whole focus is to deliver what will most benefit the young person right now.

In the late Love of Learning years, for example, around ages 11-13, a lot of youth flourish when a Mom School gives them opportunities to participate in theater, choir, science class with labs, or other activities. This creates positive peer interaction, reading and discussing of great works such as Shakespeare, Austen, or Aristotle, and fun times with friends. When a mom leads out and organizes such a class, and helps several young people and their parents in the process, it frequently creates a thriving environment of reading, discussing, and learning.

In fact, such a Mom School can also work very effectively during the Scholar Phase Practice Year. Students have time for the Practice and also the Shakespeare class and play, choir, math course or other event the mom realizes is needed.

A Mom School can also be helpful during the First Intense Reading Year, if the focus is on holding regular book discussions. In other words, the Mom announces 10 books that will be read over the course of 10-12 weeks, with a discussion about each book once a week at her home or another convenient place.

The course emphasizes books that will greatly help her child—the right topics, the right level of reading, the right group of peers. She invites peers, signs up those who want to participate, includes other parents in the implementation (if they want to be involved and are helpful), and holds the course.

Note that such a class is not usually helpful if it lasts too long (such as throughout both the First and Second Intense Reading Years). Better to hold a class for 10 weeks or so to catalyze the First Intense Reading Year, and then discontinue and let the student focus on lots of personal reading—with fewer weekly discussions. The discussions are still very important, but they shouldn't dominate the Year. The goal is to help the Scholar Phaser become an effective and voracious independent reader, not become dependent on a class structure, assignments from an adult, or planned discussions to keep him on task.

In fact, this often slows the student down just when it's time for him to be rushing full speed ahead into all the classics he can find! During this phase weekly discussions and any sort of formal class structure tends to give both parent and students the illusion of progress-through-busyness, while actually stifling the whole point of this year!

Too often the fact of given assignments and outside deadlines takes over and makes the scholar think that's all the study he needs—if he's getting the assignment done on time, he thinks he's *doing* Scholar Phase. Classes geared for this age group don't have time to cover as many classics as the student can and should realistically be cruising through during the second year.

For this reason, classes in the Second Intense Reading Year are often tragic in effect, as students and parents proudly look over a year of perfect attendance and assignment completion, which actually represent only a fraction of what could have been accomplished by a scholar who focused on happily and enthusiastically reading her guts out, rather than simply fulfilling the assignments to a class by the given deadline—even if those assignments were great classics and the discussions were really good. If you use classes in this year, make sure the mentors really understand Scholar Phase.

In any event, as good as those early Mom Schools can be during the last Love of Learning Year, or the First Intense Reading Year, they aren't the same as "The Class." If such early Mom Schools will help the student flourish, hold them. If not, wait until you feel they will really make a difference.

Whatever Mom Schools the student attends or doesn't attend in earlier years, during the Third Intense Reading Year it is incredibly effective to hold The Class. This is the most important Mom School for youth, because it can truly make the Scholar Phase great.

The Class doesn't focus on theatre, choir or other performance-based learning projects. Rather it emphasizes the key to truly high-level thinking: writing.

This is actually simpler than it sounds. When people learn to write well, they naturally learn to think well, organize their thoughts effectively, and present their ideas persuasively. They also learn to transition their education to a big-picture view, learning and studying in order to make a difference in the real world, to be able to impact the hearts, minds, and lives of other people, not just themselves. This does wonders in preparing a student to be not only more knowledgeable, but more capable and ready for his or her real mission in life.

The Class uses writing to help each student experience a drastic leap in her thinking ability and habits. When done effectively, all the student's skills greatly increase during The Class.

Details of The Class

The Class is easy to organize. Simply outline 10-12 weeks of learning, brainstorm which peers would bring the most to the table, invite them, and implement the class plan. An ideal class size is around 3-5 students and a mentor. It's okay to have up to 3 or 4 mentors, as long as they are all committed and participative each week.

The reason for the small class size is that writing is a very hands-on skill. If you have too many students, few of them will get enough one-on-one feedback. If you must have more students, divide the class into smaller groups—each with 5 or less students and a dedicated mentor or two.

The goal of this course is to teach each student how to think at a whole new level. To achieve this end, you'll want to make the class fun, read and discuss books that are moving and interesting, and keep the energy positive and upbeat. This isn't like a typical high school class. It's like the best high school or college class you ever attended, or if none of them were incredibly inspiring and world-changing, even better than any class you ever took.

Below are some thoughts on how you might outline the course—and keep in mind this is just a possible scenario. We have held a 3rd-Year Scholar Class on multiple occasions, and they all differed in certain particulars, to more specifically meet the needs of our scholar.

Week 1 (2 hour class)

- Start by sharing your love of learning, your excitement for the class, and your vision for how much fun the class will be.

- Share what my son Oliver James DeMille calls a "Transformational Model". This is something that *you* are passionate about, the most important thing you can think of to teach young people. Brainstorm the one thing you would teach them if you only had this chance before all of them (including your own child) would be flying off to another planet to colonize it and you'd never see them again. What would you "just have to teach" them? That's your lesson. It should take at least 20 minutes, but not more than an hour.

- When you are done teaching the Transformational Model, members of the class should feel excited. They should feel like they're part of something epic, part of something potentially great.

- Sample topics that can be Transformational Models include:

  - *Do Hard Things!*

  - *The Cashflow Quadrant* (see Robert Kiyosaki)

  - *20th Century Education and Careers vs. 21st Century Education and Careers* (See the Introduction and Chapter 1 of this book)

- *The Path of the Hero* (see Joseph Campbell, and also Book 2 of The Student Whisperer)

- *The 22 Great Teen Questions* (see Chapter 6 of Thomas Jefferson Education for Teens) Note that you don't have to use all 22 — pick and choose. Starting out this class with questions, where the students write their answers and then you ask for volunteers to share their answers with the group, is very effective.

- The 9 Skills from the Introduction of this book.

- The four types of education found in the Conclusion of this book.

There are many other options. Again, think of the most important thing you could teach them, and do so in a way that is new, inspirational, and epic.

• Take a break and have refreshments, food, treats.

• Hand out an outline of what will be covered each week in the class. Discuss why you are so excited about each of the weeks! Be specific and make it feel fun and amazing.

• Focus in on next week's assignment, and introduce it to them. Read a few select, moving passages from the assigned reading for next week — share why and how it moves you, and ask for input from the group. Let them talk, and reinforce the positives about things they say.

• Since next week's assignment is to read a book and come prepared to discuss it, spend some time teaching them how to take notes in a book. This is very important! Make it fun. Show them examples of how you have taken notes in the very book they'll be reading — and other books if you have some that are marked up well. In this case, a picture is worth a thousand words.

(Let them know ahead of time what book they'll need for the first and second weeks of class — so they can get a copy in time. Or, alternatively, have books there to hand out to them during Week 1.)

- The assignment for next week is to read one of the following books and come prepared to discuss it:
  - *The Five Love Languages of Teenagers* (Chapman)
  - *Thomas Jefferson Education for Teens* (DeMille and Brooks)
  - *Turn the Page* (Brady)

- You'll want to read all three of these books beforehand so you'll be ready. Mark them up with lots of notes as you go. If filling your books with handwritten notes is new to you, read *Turn the Page* first. In fact, if such note-taking is new to your students, have them read *Turn the Page* first.

- Finally, leave them with words of enthusiasm about next week's reading and class! Break a little early, if possible.

Week 2 (2 hour class)

- When the students arrive, seat them in a circle so everyone is facing each other, and then ask them what they liked most from the assigned book. Have them read the quote they loved most, and then discuss it as a group. Take turns. Let them talk. A lot. Share your ideas, but don't dominate the discussion. And get everyone involved as much as possible. This can take some getting used to, but if you as the mentor set a tone of fun sharing, and genuine interest in anything a person shares, others will take note and follow your lead.

- Tell the students right off the bat that there is a "no fighting" and "no attacking" rule. They can disagree—but only amiably. No personal attacks on other students, and no anger or undue negativity. "Keep it Fun and Positive!" is the rule. Disagree, yes. As long as it's fun and positive. If someone gets too negative, ask "Can you rephrase that in a way that's more fun and positive?" Or, "Does anyone have a way to say the same thing in a more positive way?" Usually somebody will turn it in the right direction. If not, say "I'm going to state this in a way that is more fun and positive…" Then turn the discussion in a less angry direction.

- Keep discussing for about an hour. Then take a break. Come back after the break and discuss the book for another 30 minutes or so. During the 30 minutes after the break, if the students haven't really warmed up to the discussion yet, feel free to share the main things you learned from the book. Have them turn to specific pages and quotes you already underlined or highlighted beforehand, read them aloud, or have students take turns reading aloud, and then discuss these quotes. Share why you liked them, or why they made you think, or why you disagreed with something. Then ask them to share their ideas as well. But don't do this during the first hour. Let them discuss, or be silent, but don't take over—at least not until after the break.

- The last 30 minute of class, focus on the assignment for next week. They'll be reading a second of these three books:
  - *The Five Love Languages of Teenagers* (Chapman)
  - *Thomas Jefferson Education for Teens* (DeMille and Brooks)
  - *Turn the Page* (Brady)

  Select whichever one you think will most benefit the group. Again, share what you love about the reading, have them read aloud a few quotes that you've pre-selected, and share your enthusiasm and excitement about the book.

- Finally, give them a writing assignment for next week. In addition to reading the second book, they need to write a one-page paper on something they really care about. It can be anything. If they choose to write fiction or poetry, it can be more than 1 page—as long as they want. If it's non-fiction, have them stick to 1 page. This helps them think concisely and focus on getting the important ideas onto a single page.

- Tell the students to bring a copy of their paper for each member of the class—to turn in at the beginning of class next week. In other words, if there are 5 students in the class and 2 mentors, each student needs to bring 7 copies of his/her one-page paper next week. If there are 3 students and 1 mentor, each student should bring 4 copies of his/her paper to class.

- Teach them that part of learning to write well is learning to read other people's writing and help improve it.

- Leave them with a feeling of how excited you are to read their papers and how much you love writing.

Week 3 (3 hour class)

- Start by discussing this week's reading assignment for an hour. Make it fun. Don't dominate, just keep the discussion going. If needed, the following questions almost always spark interest and discussion:

  - *What was your favorite thing in this book?*
  - *What was your favorite quote in the book?*
  - *Did you disagree with anything? What was it, and why do you disagree?*
  - *One of my favorite quotes in the book is (read a passage you've pre-selected). I love it because…   What do you guys think of it?*
  - *I don't quite understand one thing about the book. On page…, it says… I don't get it. Can anyone clarify this for me?*

  Since this is the second week of discussion, most of the students will probably be more engaged in the conversation. Again, guide them along.

  If you don't have much personal experience with such discussions, prepare by listening to some of the Mentoring in the Classics audios, available at TJEd.org/MIC. Just listening to 2-3 of these discussions will give you a sense of what great discussion can be like—and help you aim for it.

- After an hour or so, take a break.

- When you return, ask if the group wants to discuss more or move on to the next project. Let them decide. Most groups will want to discuss more. (If they're still not excited about a lot of discussion, they're probably not taking lots of good handwritten notes in their book margins as they read. Take some time to ensure that they understand and are effectively using this skill.)

- Leave at least 90 minutes for the writing section of today's class.

- With at least 90 minutes left, end the discussion and have students turn in the one-page papers they wrote, with enough copies made for everyone in the group. Distribute 1 copy of each student's paper to each person in the class—both students and mentors. Everyone should also have a pen in hand.

- Ask for a volunteer to share his or her paper with the whole class. Have everyone turn to the volunteer's paper, and have the volunteer begin reading aloud what he/she wrote. Tell him that you'll interrupt **a lot**, but to read aloud until you interrupt.

  This begins a powerful method of learning—to write, to think, and to analyze as well as increase one's creativity. As the student reads aloud, politely interrupt any time you have a suggestion. Invite the rest of the class to do the same. Politely!

  Teach them to say: "Oh, that needs a comma…" "I think 'exsception' is misspelled. It should be 'exception,' right?" The whole class carries on a dialogue, suggesting changes to the volunteer's paper. "I really love the way you said…" "I don't get what this sentence means. Can you clarify?" "Oh, that's what you meant. It's a bit unclear. How could you write it so it's more clear?"

  As a group, edit and upgrade the paper. Go slowly. Make suggestions. Fix any typos or grammatical errors. Make suggestions for organization, flow, tone, voice, word choice, audience, etc. Let everyone participate. Rule: Polite, fun, and positive!

- Have the following books on hand for reference, so when people aren't sure of a certain grammatical rule they'll be able to look it up. Have the students look things up in these books (rather than you doing it for them). Make it a fun class exercise to check things, if needed. This easily (and in a fun way) teaches them to look up grammatical rules when in doubt. The books are:

  - *The Elements of Style* (Strunk and White)
  - *The Elements of Grammar* (Shertzer)

- Keep having the volunteer read her paper aloud, and have the group give feedback and recommendations. For example, point out when something in the paper feels confusing, or not quite effective. Ask for suggestions on how to fix it. Everyone should take handwritten notes on their own copy of the volunteer's paper, practicing fixes as they go. Another example:

- *Class Member: "I think this character is…*
  kind of fake. I just don't understand him."
- *Mentor: "I don't know. I like that character. But maybe you*
  can strengthen him. Does anyone else find him a bit fake?"
- *Different Class Member: "I do. I just don't like this character…"*
- *Mentor: "How can Carrie (the Volunteer) make this character more*
  authentic? So he connects better with the reader. Any ideas?"
- *Class Member: "Well, she could have him say more — more*
  dialogue, less of the author telling us about the character and
  more of him talking. That way, we get to know him for him."
- *Carrie: "Ah. Great idea…" (Her voice trails off*
  while she's taking notes on her page.)

> This kind of writing mentoring is modeled and taught in depth and detail in our How to Mentor Course (TJEd.org/htm) — including group editing sessions recorded live, and successive drafts of papers worked on in the sessions.

- For the rest of the class period, go through the paper and engage in many conversations like this: Discussing the volunteer's paper and suggesting problems, ideas, fixes, edits. Again, keep it polite and positive. And get people involved. If one student says nothing, eventually ask him if he has any thoughts on the volunteer's paper. If not, don't push. But give him a chance.

- If you finish the volunteer's paper, ask for another volunteer. If feedback on the first paper was helpful and polite, you'll probably have lots of volunteers who want to go next. Pick the first to volunteer and start on his/her paper — using the same method.

- This method is incredibly effective. It very quickly teaches deeper thinking, the rules of punctuation and grammar (in a fun, non-rote way), and the skills of analytical, creative, and persuasive thinking and writing. And it benefits not only the person whose paper is being analyzed, but everyone who has put themselves in the mind of the writing mentor. It does so naturally, in a simulation-style environment where each student feels like she is part of something.

- At the end of class, tell everyone that next week's assignment is to make their paper even better, and longer if they want, and bring a copy of it for everyone in class. Those who volunteered and had their papers covered in class should upgrade their paper, using the feedback and ideas they just received, and everyone else should improve their papers as well. Just participating in the edits of today's volunteer papers will help them do the same thing on their own paper during the week.

- Tell them to put lots of effort into this paper. No reading assignment for next week. Just put serious work into making their paper as great as they can.

- Today, after class: read the papers from all the students who didn't get their papers discussed by the group, and add numerous positive suggestions in your handwriting right on the page. Get the paper back to each student today, so they can use your comments in their rewrite during the week. But make sure your edits are positive and helpful.

Don't mark typos or grammatical problems this time through the paper. Leave those for the class environment. Seriously! In the class, such corrections feel helpful; in contrast, a paper covered with red markings and numerous fixes often feels invasive and upsetting to beginners. But do provide ideas, praise for things well done, and whatever else you can write on their paper that will inspire them to write an even better paper for next week. Inspire them! Leave them feeling praised and uplifted—and with genuine ideas to help upgrade their next draft.

Some common feedback that I see on drafts like this include:
- *I think you would get a lot out of reading this out loud to yourself.*
- *I would pass this by a couple of readers and ask for proof-reading suggestions that are easily fixed.*
- *Do you enjoy this topic? If not, is there something that matters more deeply to you that you could write about? [How about...?]*

- *…and so forth.*

- It is amazing how many students experience a drastic improvement in their writing and thinking skills during this next week. The experience of watching a paper go through the group editing process—being questioned, probed, and infused with new ideas and suggestions—is a powerful, mind-shifting event. The neurons and neural pathways start firing in whole new ways and unexplored directions. Many young people go home and find themselves much better writers than yesterday—and much more enthusiastic writers than before.

- Sometime during this week you'll likely have a student (or several) who contact you and want to change the topic of their paper. This is a touchy situation, but it usually means that they just find it difficult to rewrite. The truth is that writing a first draft is an easy process for most students compared to rewriting and improving a paper.

If a student doesn't contact you, but just switches topics and brings a new paper next week, roll with it. He went through the process and you can focus on helping him improve his current draft. But if he asks for permission to switch subjects, try to get him to stick with the original topic. Most young people need a lot of practice in the skills of rewriting, not pumping out first drafts.

The best way to handle this is usually to be disappointed— but in a very positive way. "Tommy, I was so excited with your paper. I love what you wrote, and I would be so disappointed not to see you really make that paper great. You've got a fantastic start, and it's such an important [or interesting] topic. I hope you'll finish it before doing another topic. We'll have time for another topic later in this class. And with such a great start on your paper already, I hate to see you start over. I want to see what you can do with such an excellent paper."

If he switches topics after this, fine. But try to get him to push through, if possible. The truth is that if he writes on a new topic he'll almost certainly compose it at the same level as last week's submission. If he rewrites last week's paper, on the other hand, he'll experience real improvement. And that's the more important lesson.

Still, his enthusiasm is the most important thing at this point, so leave the final decision up to him.

Week 4 (3 hour class)

- Have all the students pass out copies of their papers, and repeat the writing workshop from last week. Ask for volunteers— start with those who didn't get to have their papers discussed last week—and get through as many papers as you can.

- Make this fun. Take breaks as needed. Don't rush. Take the time to respond to each paper well, word-for-word, read aloud with feedback from the whole class. Keep it positive, polite, and fun. And be vocally enthusiastic. Get authentically excited about each paper, and each student. Show them your love of their ideas, their thinking, and the ways they express things in writing.

- Spend the entire class editing as a group, and make it enjoyable. If things get bogged down or boring, take a quick 3 minutes and share an important quote or big idea that you prepared before class (come with 5 or 6 of these, but don't use them unless they are needed). Just read the quote, share why you are moved by it, and ask them their thoughts.

  This is a mini-discussion, and it reinforces the lesson of discussing important things while also keeping their minds engaged and interested. If you don't have any ideas of what to share here, use quotes from the books you haven't yet covered in class. Or study Zeno's paradoxes, or anything in the margins of the excellent book *A Beginner's Guide to Constructing the Universe* (Schneider). With a little preparation of this sort, you can keep things interesting even if the editing gets a bit dry.

- At the end of class, introduce the assignment for next week, which is to put their papers aside for the week and read. Choose a book for Week 5 that will really spark the imagination, and lead to lots of fun discussion next week. Here are a few that typically work well:

- *Mistborn* (Sanderson)
- *Pawn of Prophecy* (Eddings)
- *Bendigo Shafter* (L'Amour)
- *Animal Farm* (Orwell)
- *The Chosen* (Potok)

Note that these titles assume your class participants are 15 or older. Younger students will likely do better with books such as:
- *Carry On, Mr. Bowditch* (Latham)
- *The Great Brain* (Fitzgerald)
- *Trumpet of the Swan* (White)
- *The Lion, the Witch, and the Wardrobe* (Lewis)
- *Little House in the Big Woods* (Wilder)

• At the end of class, have everyone turn in the copies of any student papers you haven't yet covered as a class. Keep these with you and bring them next week to pass out again and use in class.

• Leave everyone with a feeling of excitement about next week's reading!

Week 5 (3 hour class)

• Spend the first half of class using the same process of group feedback to any student papers that haven't yet been read aloud and discussed by everyone.

• Use the second half of class to discuss the assigned book.

• Leave everyone with a feeling of enthusiasm about next week's class.

Weeks 6-12 (3 hours each)

• By this point you'll have the hang of things. Give writing assignments, and especially re-writing assignments. It's best to let students improve just one paper, or start a second and spend the rest of the class on that one if they choose. Taking one paper and making it the best the student possibly can is much more effective than doing a bunch of different papers on different topics or formats. One paper—and greatly improved, week after week!

That's what class is all about. It brings real depth,
and truly improves skills. That's the purpose.

- Some weeks students should write. Some weeks they should read.
  Some weeks assign both. During class, discuss what they've read,
  and keep working in the group format to read student papers and
  suggest edits and improvements. Over and over. Have each student
  go through multiple drafts of her paper—always improving it.

- Here is a list of books highly recommended for reading
  and discussing during The Class (of course, only
  choose a few and really go deep with each):

  - *The Five Love Languages of Teenagers* (Chapman)
  - *Thomas Jefferson Education for Teens* (DeMille and Brooks)
  - *Turn the Page* (Brady)
  - *Mistborn* (Sanderson)
  - *Pawn of Prophecy* (Eddings)
  - *Bendigo Shafter* (L'Amour)
  - *Animal Farm* (Orwell)
  - *The Chosen* (Potok)
  - *Carry On, Mr. Bowditch* (Latham)
  - *The Great Brain* (Fitzgerald)
  - *Trumpet of the Swan* (White)
  - *The Lion, the Witch, and the Wardrobe* (Lewis)
  - *Little House in the Big Woods* (Wilder)
  - *LeaderShift* (Woodward and DeMille)
  - *The Power of Four* (Marshall)
  - *The Phantom Tollbooth* (Juster)
  - *Anne of Green Gables* (Montgomery)
  - *The Cricket in Times Square* (Seldon and Williams)
  - *Tom Sawyer* (Twain)
  - *We Hold These Truths to Be Self-Evident* (DeMille)
  - *The Rithmatist* (Sanderson)
  - *A Beginner's Guide to Constructing the Universe* (Schneider)
  - *Rascal* (Brady)
  - *Pollyanna* (Porter)
  - *Resolved* (Woodward)
  - *The Science of Getting Rich* (Wattles)

      - *Elantris* (Sanderson)

      - *Financial Fitness for Teens* (Brady)

      - *The Alchemist* (Coelho)

- If a student has already read some or all of these books before The Class, that's great. Teach them to re-read, and emphasize that this is ideal; make sure they know that they'll learn much more the second or third time through a book.

- Strike a balance between reading books and discussing them as a class on the one hand, and on the other hand re-writing and spending class time giving group feedback to student papers. Do a little more writing than reading.

Overall Class Plan

Note: The Class is usually most effective when it begins in early fall and ends before the holiday season. You can do it other times, but most people find that students give more effort and stay more focused during this time of the year than others.

Once you have completed this 10-12 week course, The Class is half done. The second half follows a similar format (usually 10-12 weeks, beginning in January). In this course, assign 3-5 books to read, no more than 5, and spend a lot of time on the writing. Have each student pick a new topic and spend the whole 10-12 week class improving that one multi-page paper—and upgrading it week after week, with frequent class feedback. (The exception is if a student is writing a novel or a full book, in which case let him continue it from the fall class and keep working on it through winter.)

At this point members of the class will be very skilled at providing feedback during the group discussion of student writings, and the more time you spend on this the better they'll become. Student writing will drastically improve, and keep improving. This is a powerful process that will set a tone of quality for each student's whole education. The Class is profound, and it works.

In the second 10-12 weeks, there is one very important addition. The students will read and discuss great books, and they'll write and provide mutual feedback on each other's writing. In addition, it's very helpful to spend the last 4 weeks on public speaking. Use the book *SPLASH!: A Leader's Guide to Effective Public Speaking* (Brady), or another book on public speaking that is just as good, and make it the last book they read. Spend one class period discussing it in detail as a group.

Then use the last 3 weeks of class having students stand and deliver speeches—of 10 minutes or less—followed by perhaps 20 minutes of feedback and positive suggestions from members of the class. This takes what they've learned from the reading and writing portions of the course and bumps it to a whole new level.

When a student has completed the 6 months of The Class as outlined, he/she will be at a much higher plane of intellect, maturity, and thinking-writing-analytical-creative-teamwork-speaking skills. The Class is powerful.

Intense Reading Rules!

During The Class, and the rest of the Third Intense Reading Year, it is important not to let up on focused reading, note taking, and discussing. The Class is meant to be a supplement to, not a replacement for, the Third Intense Reading Year. Students should be reading, reading, reading before The Class, during the weeks of The Class, and after The Class is complete.

Indeed, the deeper level of thinking that students naturally develop during The Class will only improve how much is learned in daily reading, and by this point they likely have the maturity and the drive to continue reading multiple things aside from class assignments, without getting distracted. This Year is mostly about Intense Reading, with The Class adding a way to deepen and improve each student's knowledge, learning skills, and learning ability.

Finally, there is no doubt that mentoring The Class is a major project for the Mom, Dad, teacher, or whoever serves as the main class mentor(s). But unlike many educational projects that are taxing yet don't seem to bear much fruit in the intellectual life of each student, The Class nearly always changes everything. Students who have done it almost universally consider it the most important part of their education—the turning point where they truly learned to think and learn greatly. And parents who have done it nearly all comment on how much fun it was. They love it.

The Class, when done effectively, is one of those great educational experiences that feel like…well, it's hard to explain. If you've ever attended a youth conference and had a life-changing experience full of epiphanies and mind-opening interactions, that's what The Class feels like—except you don't go home after 2 or 3 days. The feeling of flow, excitement, and great self-improvement lasts for months—and it changes you forever. This is just as true of parents as it is for their youth.

The truth is, the teacher really does learn more than the student. And when moms/dads do The Class with their kids, they have one of the most fantastic educational experiences of their lives. Parents who have done The Class routinely find themselves wishing the next child were already prepared for The Class—so they could bask in the same powerful energy of great learning every year!

But don't! When the 5-6 months of The Class are over, help your student re-focus on even more reading, reading, reading—even more than while The Class was in session. Such reading is where truly great education happens. This is especially true after the greatly expanded learning and skills each student gains from The Class.

8
Year Four

"Thou shalt never get such a secret from me but by a parable."
−SHAKESPEARE

*"Sometimes something is so important to human knowledge,
that God will only teach it through a classic."*
−HANDWRITTEN NOTES ON TWO GENTLEMEN OF VERONA

THE main purpose of this year is by now quite familiar: read, read more, and study in all fields of learning, take notes, discuss, and read even more. The Fourth Year of such reading is a time for serious breadth, depth, and a great deal of thinking and learning. Indeed, the 5,000 hours of Scholar Phase are rounded out in this Fourth Year of Intense Reading.

While each individual student gets a personalized education in this type of learning, in general the reading, discussing, studying, and projects break down in the pattern outlined in the Study Overview textbox on the next page.

Of course, the reading hours listed here are conservative. A student who wants to read more can amass 5,000 hours of reading, note taking, discussing, studying and all the learning that goes with it in a much shorter period.

Compare this to an average high school "study and read rate" of 3 hours a day during the school year (this is higher than the actual average). This doesn't include time sitting in class, which is largely unproductive for most students in terms of truly learning. At 3 hours of quality reading, deep studying, and discussing a day for a typical 180-day public school year, that's 540 hours of study a year, or 2,160 hours in four years of high school. That's less than half a Scholar Phase, even assuming the materials read are of the highest quality found in the Great Books and others like them.

Also, the 2,160 hours would only actually count toward Scholar Phase if they were completed using the Discussion Method of Learning (the Oxford, Cambridge, and American founding era tradition of learning *how* to think) rather than the Lecture Method (the Germanic approach of teaching *what* to think). In any case, what passes for education in many modern school settings isn't on par with true Scholar Phase learning—qualitatively or quantitatively.

Parents and youth can of course supplement such schooling with Scholar Phase learning in The Greats. The focus shouldn't be on hours, per se, but on the quality of learning—both in terms of knowledge and gaining of important skills. But the sample below does help provide a rough guideline for how many hours a day Scholar Phasers should aim for during each of the Years of Scholar Phase.

Year	Study Overview	Total Hours
Practice Year	5 hours a day, 4 days a week, 10 months of the year = 800 hours	800
First Intense Reading Year	5 hours a day, 5 days a week, 10 months of the year = 1000 hours	1,800
Second Intense Reading Year	6 hours a day, 5 days a week, 10 months of the year = 1200 hours	3,000
Third Intense Reading Year/ The Class	8 hours a day, 5 days a week, 10 months of the year = 1600 hours	4,600
Fourth Intense Reading Year/ The Bridge	8 hours a day, 5 days a week, 10 months of the year = 1600 hours	6,200

Ideally, Scholar Phasers will engage increasing study hours each year, and go well beyond the minimums outlined in the sample above. Of course, it is crucial to personalize the education of each student to his/her specific needs. This kind of individualized learning is often the difference between great education and more mediocre approaches to schooling.

Students who read many or all of the 400 books listed in Chapter 6, and numerous other great works at the same level of quality, along with math, science, language, religious works, online tutorials on interesting topics, and other areas of study—using the Discussion Method of learning—will obtain a great education. The Fourth Intensive Reading Year is a time to notice any gaps and fill them in. If the student hasn't read or studied much about chemistry, for example, or the arts and art history, etc., this is the time to read up on that topic and gain the necessary knowledge and skills.

In addition, the Fourth Intense Reading Year also provides a time to boost one's base of knowledge and prepare for nationalized exams (if desired). This is called "The Bridge." (Get an audio download of "The Bridge" where I explain this in more detail, at TJEd.org/Bridge.) Reading is still the focus, and this should be supplemented with what we call The Cards.

The Cards

To excel in this project, each student needs access to the following books (or online equivalents):

- *The Timetables of History* (Grun)
- *The Dictionary of Cultural Literacy* (Hirsch)
- *Noah Webster's 1828 Dictionary*
- SAT/ACT Study Manuals (or online tutorials)

The process is very simple. The goal is to fill one's mind with important facts, a survey of human knowledge on a surface level: dates, formulas, etc. These data serve as a cognitive "peg board" that helps with fluency and rapport in recognizing and discussing new ideas, in making correlations and connections, in understanding context, allusions and references, and in laying a foundation for future learning on the topics covered, with greater depth and focus. Memorization is often overdone in the modern

Lecture Approach to education, but it has an exceedingly important place in The Bridge.

During the Fourth Intense Reading Year, memorize a great deal. A good place to start is with *The Dictionary of Cultural Literacy*. Some Scholar Phasers simply memorize the cursory details of every entry in this Dictionary—including the math, science, history, language, and everything else. Having this much information at ready is extremely valuable. It isn't as important as knowing how to think, but knowing how to think and also having a trove of factual knowledge stored in your mind is a great combination. Yes, a lot of people will have such knowledge quickly available online, but you'll have it in your memory—and learning it will make you a better thinker/analyzer/utilizer of knowledge.

Waiting until the student is more mature and has a lot of reading, writing, thinking and discussing under her belt is extremely important, so that 1) she doesn't learn to rely on memorization as a substitute for thinking and learning and 2) she has a context of experience and a reservoir of reading that make the factoids meaningful and relevant. That way they're not stored as factoids in some data-retrieval fashion that only works for test-taking. The things memorized in late Scholar Phase will have connections, correlations and context based on previous learning, and will serve as magnetic points of attraction so that future learning will be more meaningful and relevant.

One of the simplest ways to get the information into your memory is to use The Cards. People with a photographic memory can just read and remember. For the rest of us, The Cards are extremely effective.

Here's how they work. Get packages of 3x5 cards from the store or order them online. Open *The Dictionary of Cultural Literacy* to the Contents page and read over the chapter topics. Select a chapter that is interesting to you, and start there.

Turn to the chapter, and read the first entry. Then the next. Read all the entries on the first page of the chapter. Then summarize them on The Cards—with one to two prompt-lines per entry, rather than a whole paragraph of details.

If you prefer to begin with historical dates, rather than *The Dictionary of Cultural Literacy*, this is just as effective. Simply go to the beginning of *The Timetables of History* and begin studying the earliest years. Or pick a time period (such as the 8th Century B.C. or the 13th Century A.D.) and begin learning what happened during that era.

Whatever topic you're studying, begin putting information on The Cards. Write a question or keyword on one side of a card, and an answer on the other side. For example, let's say you're learning about early American history. You decide to learn the important dates of major events. So, on one side of the card you write:

    1776?

On the other side you give the answer:

    The Declaration of Independence

Of course, there's a lot more to know about 1776 than just that The Declaration came that year. But this gives you the date of a very important event. To round it out, add more to the first side of the card:

    1770?

    1771?

    1772?

    1773?

    1774?

    1775?

    1776?

    1777?

    1778?

    1779?

On the other side:

    1770—The Boston Massacre

    1771—New York Hospital founded

    1772—Samuel Adams forms Committees of Correspondence

1773—Boston Tea Party

1774—British close the Port of Boston

1775—Paul Revere's ride, Lexington and Concord, Second Continental Congress

1776—George Washington and troops fight British, Declaration of Independence

1777—Lafayette helps Washington

1778—France allies with the Colonies

1779—Spain declares war on Britain

There is a special added benefit when you make these cards yourself by writing things in your own handwriting. This actually helps your memory.

Now, once you've made your first card, it's fairly easy to memorize the information it contains. Sit down and go through it 10 times: read the question, then try to remember the answer. If you remember, turn the card over to see if you got it right. If you can't remember, turn the card over to see what the answer is. Do this repeatedly with each question.

After 10 times through the card, trying to remember each answer—then checking to see if you got it right—you'll likely remember more than half of the answers. Great. Time to make a new card.

1780?

1781?

1782?

1783?

1784?

1785?

1786?

1787?

1788?

1789?

Now add answers to the other side of the card:

1780—Benedict Arnold discovered to be a traitor

1781—British surrender to Americans in land war, but keep attacking American shipping

1782—Benjamin Franklin negotiates with British for a lasting peace

1783—Britain recognizes American independence

1784—Thomas Jefferson's land ordinance passed

1785—James Madison's religious freedom act passes

1786—Annapolis Convention held, led by Madison and Hamilton

1787—Constitutional Convention held, Constitution written

1788—U.S. Constitution ratified by 9th state (New Hampshire) and goes into effect, New York made the first capital of the U.S.

1789—first U.S. president George Washington, first U.S. Congress meets in New York, the French Revolution begins

If you need more than one card to write your answers, use two. Or however many it takes to do the job.

Also, as you are writing down the answers, read about the ones that are completely new or foreign to you. You'll never memorize effectively if you have no earthly idea what it's talking about. For example, if you find that the Annapolis Convention was held in 1786 and led by Madison and Hamilton, but you don't know anything about the Annapolis Convention, look it up and find out the details. The purpose of this entire project is primarily *learning*—while memorizing facts is only secondary. When it comes to the memorization portion, don't try to make the content on The Cards too detailed! You really are just committing factoids to memory.

If you have a sense of purpose in a particular subject area and you want to be more conversant in minor details, make a card just about this one topic. On one side:

Annapolis Convention?

On the other side of the card list several important details you've learned about this event that will help you remember. Create extra cards like these on any questions/answers where you feel the need to remember more about the details. The cards make learning easy, but you have to write down things you want or need to remember and get them on a card.

Once you've finished writing these second and third cards, go through them 10 times and try to remember each answer. Do this every time you make a new card: write the questions and answers, then immediately try 10 times to answer each question.

As noted, in addition to the dates and events, you can add even more depth to this by including extra cards that help you remember even more about a given item. For example, you've listed "The U.S. Constitution" as an answer for "1787?" But you can go even deeper with an additional card:

U.S. Constitution, Article I?

Article 2?

Article 3?

Article 4?

Article 5?

Article 6?

Article 7?

Article 8?

Answers:

1-Legislative Branch

2-Executive Branch

3-Judicial Branch

4-The States

5-Amending Process

6-Supremacy

7-Ratification

8-There is no Article 8!

If you aren't sure you fully understand something, such as the Amending Process or Supremacy, make a card with those as the questions and more details in the answers. Once you've written these cards, go through each

INTENSE READING YEAR 4 + THE BRIDGE

10 times. Then put them in your stack with the other cards you've made. Do this any time you want to know more about a fact or detail.

When you have made as many cards as you plan to make right now, spend some time memorizing them. Pull out your stack of cards and start going through each question—trying to remember the answer. If you remember an answer, great. If not, re-read the questions and answers 5 times each to let repetition boost your memory.

Do this all the way through your stack of cards. Then do it again. And again. When you make several cards in a day, take the time to memorize them as much as you can that very same day. Take them with you to town, to your room, when you go jogging, everywhere. Keep them with you, and pull them out and memorize them repeatedly every day. As your stack grows, keep memorizing. Take the cards with you every day and memorize them during any down time you might have, sitting and waiting for something. In addition, have some focused, dedicated time planned in your weekly schedule for Cards memorization and review.

Next Level

When you feel that you know the answers on a card quite well, get out a pen and give yourself a mini-quiz. Go through each question, and see if you remember the answer. If you do, use your pen to put a dot • next to the item. If you know all the answers on a card, it will have dots on every question. If not, you'll have some items with dots and others without. Keep testing yourself this way every time you come to the same card in your stack.

When you reach 4 dots on a given item (meaning that you've quizzed yourself 4 different times and got the correct answer each time), you can skip it from now on—just focusing on the other questions that you haven't fully memorized yet. For example, at some point your card may look like this:

     1780? •••

     1781? •••

     1782? ••••

     1783? ••••

1784? ••••

1785? ••••

1786? ••

1787? ••••

1788? ••••

1789? ••••

Next time you come back to this card, practice memorizing the answers for 1781 and 1786. Skip the rest.

At any given point, you might have a stack of 30 cards, but only be memorizing 36 total items—because you already know the rest of the answers on all the cards. Or you may need to memorize more, or less. The important thing is to keep memorizing, and keep making more cards.

As you practice, sometimes use the answer side of each card to ask yourself questions, and see if you get the dates right (or whatever is on the question side of the card). Also, at times start questioning yourself from the bottom of the card, instead of the top, or from the middle of the card. And at times have someone quiz you by picking questions randomly from each card, in no particular order. This helps you learn the answers without relying on the normal order.

The Cards work for studying chemistry, biology, math formulas and proofs, history, grammatical rules, and so on. It works for pretty much anything. If you are preparing for an essay exam, for example, you can put Part I as the question on one side of a card, and a list of things you want to write in your essay on the other side of the card. Then make a card for Part II, Part III, and so on. This system allows you to quickly and simply memorize a great deal of information.

You can even list your question as "Memorized Shakespeare Quote #1", and have the quote on the answer side of the card. This allows you to memorize many things, and be ready with quick recall whenever you need it. Save your stack of cards, and at the end of this learning Year you can pull them all out and quickly review them. Put a mark by any answers you don't remember, and spend more time memorizing those answers. You'll very quickly recall everything in your stack of cards.

Again, this system allows you to amass great amounts of factual knowledge—and almost everyone gets better at it as they do more of it. You can literally stuff your mind with a great deal of knowledge, facts, and details that you'll remember for a long time. Don't cram. Memorize over time so you'll remember the things you learn. And keep your cards, long-term, in a card file so you can go back and review past cards from time to time, on a planned schedule—say, once every month you pull out the oldest x-number of cards and review them.

During the Fourth Intense Reading Year, fill your memory with as many bits and bytes of knowledge as you can. *The Dictionary of Cultural Literacy* makes this even easier by putting thousands of factoids all in one easy-to-access place.

As I mentioned previously, in modern education we too often overemphasize memorization, but that doesn't mean that we should ignore it. We shouldn't make it the focus of 12 years of rote schooling, but putting some real effort into memorizing a number of important things during this Year will greatly boost the quality of your learning. Knowledge matters. Not as much as being able to think—but you can have both, if the balance and process are executed thoughtfully and in harmony with your big-picture goals for Scholar Phase and beyond. The Cards make this simple and relatively easy.

Use The Cards on every topic, and learn the important information that will prepare you to better understand the world and things you will experience in adult life. Knowledge is power—and memorization with The Cards is a powerful technology. It really works.

Test Prep

As you become increasingly proficient with The Cards and memorize more and more facts, along with continued great reading and discussions, you'll eventually see how useful The Cards can be in test prep. When it is appropriate, take several sample SAT or ACT exams, or equivalent for your nation, and see how you do. Use practice guides (available in print and online) to find out how you can improve your test scores, and use The Cards to easily and quickly boost your vocabulary, mental reservoir of factual knowledge, and testing abilities.

Do as much as you need to repeatedly score very high on the practice exams. The Cards will help, if you use them.

The Cards can be adapted to anything, really—at least to anything where memorization is helpful. For example, make cards that help you memorize the Periodic Table, the main points in each of the 85 essays from *The Federalist Papers*, the amino acids in the human body, the dates of each U.S. president in history, the plot of every Shakespeare play, the basic geometric proofs and formulas and how to apply them, etc. The sky is the limit. Actually—it's not. There is no limit!

In addition, there are several topics (like Art History, Geography, or Anatomy, for example) where a 3x5 card isn't the best tool, but the system of The Cards is still very effective. Specifically, get colored or black-and-white prints of great historical works of art, architecture, sculpture, etc., and write dates, artists, and details on the back; or a diagram of the bones in the human body that allows you to fill in the name of each bone. Or go to online geography or anatomy sites that have you enter the names of countries, capital cities, rivers, mountain ranges, etc. on a blank map or electronic equivalent.

The system of such games or projects is based on the same methodology as The Cards—you look at a blank map, diagram, or painting, and provide answers and details about each through repetition and memory building. This works. It is an important part of learning.

Again, many young people are taught to memorize before they learn how to think, and this often conditions them to use rote memory *instead* of developing deep analytical, creative, or innovative thinking skills. But by reading the greats and using the Discussion Method of learning, you gain deep and effective thinking skills—and the addition of memorized facts and knowledge only strengthens your thinking abilities. Both are needed. Learning how to think should come first. Then, later, The Cards greatly improve the process of learning everything you want and need to know.

To get started, follow the plan outlined earlier in this chapter: Pick a chapter from *The Dictionary of Cultural Literacy* and use The Cards to memorize every entry. Then do the same with a second chapter, and then memorize all entries in the entire *Dictionary of Cultural Literacy*, to the extent you and your mentor find advantageous to your personal goals. Add historical dates, mathematical formulas and proofs, and other knowledge worth memorizing to the process. This system not only greatly expands your store of memorized knowledge, but it will give you a number of very important new learning skills in the process.

Have fun with it. Turn it into a game, and find ways to make it enjoyable. We have used a Trivial Pursuit set, assigning each color of token to a particular chapter in the *Dictionary of Cultural Literacy*, and played teams to quiz the content for the win. Fun!

The Cards are power. Use them! As you create more and more cards, put them in a file or a dedicated drawer. You want a great education, and The Cards can really help. Indeed, repeated memorization will upgrade your memorization skills in general.

In all of this, keep reading great things and discussing much of what you read. Take quality notes, read more, discuss. Over and over. Scholar Phase is the crux of a great education.

Timing for Parents (and Mentors)

Occasionally a student wants to do The Cards before The Class. We have introduced the learning order the way it is in this book because most young people benefit by experiencing The Class before they engage an in-depth (and usually individual) study using The Cards. But it is fine to reverse this order if a student feels excited about The Cards and wants to do them without waiting for The Class. It is important to personalize the learning of each student.

In fact, we've seen excellent results with a few students who decided to do The Class and The Cards at the same time. It turned into a class competition to memorize as much as possible, and this added to the experiences of writing and discussing great books. It didn't detract—it made The Class even better.

Consider what your teen needs, and get her involved in reading this book and helping make important decisions about what is next in her own education.

We live in a world where many adults want their kids to "get ahead" as quickly as possible. There is a subtle but strong pressure on many young people to do things earlier and younger—as if this will somehow make them better. It is important to resist this tendency, and to discuss this kind of pressure with each youth. She should know that "doing it younger isn't better." The truth is that "better is better," and doing things at the best time for a specific student will always bring better results. It's not a race.

Quality is the goal, not speed, or even timeline.

In short, teach young people to go at their optimal pace. Once they are in Scholar Phase, teach them to push themselves, but even pushing themselves is most effective when done at their own pace. In practical terms, this means that if a student begins The Cards earlier than the Fourth Intense Reading Year but starts to dislike the project, it's okay to back off. It's often wise in such circumstances to put off The Cards until a later date.

Most 17- or 18-year-olds are excited to really push beyond their comfort zone, but a few aren't. In truth, if a 17- or 18-year-old is struggling this way, he probably hasn't done the 5,000 hours of great reading and discussing.

In such cases, his best focus is to keep working on his 5,000 hours. Once he has the hours under his belt, however, it's time to push hard and memorize a lot of knowledge. The Cards make this easier, and while they are hard work, the rate of increased learning makes the process fun for almost everyone. If it isn't fun (for such a student), he usually needs to work harder at it. He can do hard things.

As always, individualize, taking into account important factors such as learning styles, interest levels, developmental anomalies, etc. Great education is personalized.

BOOK THREE

IMPACT ON SOCIETY

"…we were born yesterday, but the world wasn't. All that we learn as we grow up is selected from what was discovered or invented in the past, sometimes the very remote past. Our most cherished ideas and social attitudes were formulated by those who lived before us…. The American twenty-five cent piece bears the inscription 'Liberty,' a Classical [Greek] ideal, on the same side of the coin as the Hebraic 'In God We Trust.'"

–ROD W. HORTON & VINCENT F. HOPPER

"My father had talked to me as though I were a grown man, discussing not only our bookish interests, but others….talk of politics in foreign lands, of wars, battles, and courtly intrigue, of music, art, and letters…. He read me from the writings of Homer when I was very young, and from Virgil too. He taught me much of history, and not of our country only, but others as well. We talked much together, and he instructed me…. We also talked with visitors…."

–TATTON CHANTRY (LOUIS L'AMOUR)

9

The Multiple-Choice Test

"Many different meanings have been given to the word poetry.
It would weary my readers if I were to discuss which of these definitions
ought to be selected. I prefer telling them at once that which I have chosen.
In my opinion, Poetry is the search after, and the delineation of, the Ideal."

−ALEXIS DE TOCQUEVILLE, DEMOCRACY IN AMERICA

Is Star Wars poetry? Is it a search for the Ideal?
Is that what our TV shows and movies are all about—
and one of the reasons they are so popular?

−EMMA COX (HANDWRITTEN MARGIN NOTES IN DEMOCRACY IN AMERICA)

I was halfway through the meal in a crowded Los Angeles restaurant when it happened. I glanced up and noticed a man staring at me from the next table. I wondered what he was staring at, so I smiled. He grinned back, then began scrutinizing his napkin. Yes…his napkin.

I was so surprised that I watched him for a minute, and I soon realized what was going on. His napkin was spread out on the table like a large place mat. In fact, his whole family had their napkins arranged as place mats, with their plates, cups, and utensils all on top of the napkins. Together their napkins covered the whole table in a makeshift tablecloth.

The man had seen me using my napkin on the corner of my mouth—and it had shocked him. I imagine him thinking: "What kind of people use their place mats on their mouth?"

By this point he was explaining the situation to his family members, all of whom were pointing around the room at other people using their napkins as…well, napkins. Not place mats. They were speaking in a language I didn't understand, so I couldn't tell what they were saying about their new discovery.

Soon they began laughing, and somewhat sheepishly they lifted their cups and plates, moved the napkins from their position laid out on the table, and put them in their laps like napkins. It was clear that they considered this a very strange custom.

The same day my wife asked me what I would say to people who wonder why elementary and high school age homeschoolers who take standardized exams often test way above average in some areas but below them in others. I thought it was a poignant question, and it brought to mind a friendly conversation I once had with a school principal.

Culture Shock

We served on a charitable committee together, and one day in a moment of waiting he mentioned that homeschoolers in his district who, for whatever reason, take the district's standardized tests nearly all test "off the charts" high in Language Arts and Social Studies, but under the curve in Science and Math.

Then he cocked his head to one side and said, "Except for two homeschooling families in the district whose kids test the exact opposite—very high in Math and Science, and quite low in Language Arts and Social Studies." He wondered why this trend was so prominent. Why didn't they test to the averages, like most of the students?

I had just about the same reaction to him that I did to the man in the restaurant with his family's napkins under their plates. How do you tell somebody from one culture what a very different culture is like? Certainly not easily, simply, or quickly. There's more to it than that.

Still, I tried. First I referred him to national statistics that show the average of public school students (tested across the board on academic topics) in the 50th percentile, private school students in the eighties, and homeschoolers in the nineties.

As I remember it, he shook his head and said: "I've researched all those statistics, and they don't hold up because the public school numbers represent all students in public school while not all homeschoolers decide to take such tests. If we made the same tests voluntary in public schools, we'd get much higher results too—because most of those who would take them would be well prepared."

That made sense to me, so I tried another response. "Good point. The truth is that many homeschoolers don't really respect multiple-choice testing. It's not the best way to know what students have really learned. Essay exams are much better. And oral exams are even more effective. You can really explore a student's learning with oral exams."

He nodded his head vigorously. "I agree. But that isn't an option for most public schools. We are required by law to use standardized tests, most of which are multiple-choice. Parents, teachers, and administrators have little say about that. And we spend a lot of our time teaching to the mandated tests."

I asked, "Do you think you could greatly improve testing and learning if you and your teachers could design the tests yourselves instead of having to teach to those mandated?"

"Absolutely!" he suddenly got passionate about the topic.

I replied: "Well, that's exactly what many homeschooling parents are doing. They are designing the kind of assessment they think best measures what they want to emphasize in their kids' education. That's why some families excel in Math and others in Language Arts, because they have different values, goals, interests, and objectives."

He pondered, then nodded. "That makes sense. But what about the students who don't do well in certain important subjects? What do homeschoolers do about this?"

"Well, each homeschooling family does its own thing. There's not one universal way. But what do public schools do with students who don't do well in Writing, Math, Science, or some other topic?" I asked. "Or do *all* public school students excel in *every* subject?"

He grinned good-naturedly. "Touché," he said. Then his face turned serious. "But at least we try. When a student is behind in a field of study, we work hard to try to help the student catch up. Do homeschoolers do this?"

I laughed. Still chuckling, I replied, "No, not at all. Homeschoolers tell their kids to avoid subjects like Math and English and never try to learn such topics under any circumstances…" I struggled for the right way to finish my joke.

He chuckled before I could complete my thought. "Of course they try. I didn't mean to offend. It's just that my main experience with homeschoolers comes when a family stops homeschooling and their kids enter public school—and their assessment tests show them low in some area."

I nodded. "That *would* be frustrating. But like you said earlier, they are usually very high in some other topics, right?"

"Yes, nearly always."

I responded: "But homeschoolers aren't the only ones like that, right? I mean, do you have students who have been in public school their whole life, who test high in one or two topics and low in others?"

He smiled and sighed. "I see your point. Of course many students test high in some subjects and low in others."

"I bet certain students test high in most or even all subjects, and some test low in all topics. And many test in the middle on everything. Right?"

"Yes, of course," he replied.

"So, really, it's exciting when any student tests high in *anything*, right? You should be really happy with any homeschooler or public schooler, or private schooler, who comes into your school testing high in anything. Right?"

He laughed. "Conservatively optimistic, yes," he said. "But we would like them all to test high in everything."

"So would pretty much all homeschooling parents, I think," I said. "But a lot of homeschoolers are more interested in their students truly excelling and learning 'off the charts' in some important topics, so they may spend more time on those areas of focus. That would explain the high scores in subjects they care about a lot."

We both nodded. Then I chuckled again, and said, "Maybe the homeschoolers who test low in Math and Science should take classes at public school and the public school students who test low in Language Arts and Social Studies should attend some of the local homeschools."

He grinned widely. "I'd have a hard time selling that one."

"So would I," I replied.

We both laughed.

It was an interesting conversation. I felt like I really understood his views on the topic much better than before, and I think he understood mine as well. In fact, it was a lot like the man's napkin at the restaurant in L.A.

The truth is, those nice cloth napkins really did make good place mats. How sad it would have been if I'd started criticizing using the "napkin" that way and the man had started lecturing me on using my "place mat" wrongly. I'm glad we both smiled and understood each other instead—even with the cultural divide.

We each had different goals with those napkins, but they both worked. We both met our goals.

And that's the real issue, after all. If a public school meets a given family's goals for a certain child, excellent! Who is anybody else to tell those parents they should make changes? Or if a homeschool plan meets your goals for a child, why should anyone else have the right to change your way of doing things?

And this brings us to the deeper problem. The real challenge: Do you know your family's educational goals for each child? If not, that's a real problem.

That's where the "Brainstorm a Blank Page" habit comes in, as discussed in our book *The 5 Habits of Successful Homeschoolers*. To summarize, effective parent mentors sit down each week, put the name of a student they are mentoring at the top of a blank page, and brainstorm what this student needs from the mentor in the coming week. Then they repeat with each student. Week after week. The power of mentoring is real.

This really matters. If you know the right individual goals and objectives for your children and youth this week, and every week, you'll know how to make excellent decisions regarding their education. Will your insights and plans always be spot on? Well, mine aren't. Sometimes the best-laid plans don't turn out how you expected. Sometimes you'll kind of blow it. Nevertheless, just by virtue of being the kind of mentor who asks these questions, week in and week out, who analyzes her effectiveness, who considers the individual needs of each mentee— 1) you will do far better than if you weren't asking these questions; 2) sometimes (often) you'll absolutely NAIL it; and 3) over time, you'll get better and better and better at it.

But back to our main topic. Let's be clear: Testing is secondary, or more accurately, tertiary, to learning. Learning is the real goal of quality education. And different kinds of learning naturally resonate with different kinds of testing. But the starting point isn't testing. Not at all. It is knowing the right objectives right now for each child's education.

Knowing these objectives—really knowing them—will tell you how he or she should learn and how his or her learning can be most effectively tested or assessed. This is the key place to start the education of every child, and it is ultimately the responsibility of each child's parents.

Some parents delegate this duty or just leave it to someone else. But we should all celebrate parents who don't delegate this profound role in society. We need many more such parents.

The truth is that different great parents use different educational venues for their kids. Not all families that homeschool do a great job, and not all families that public school or private school always excel at parenting. Every group has its highs and lows.

With that said, it is important to remember that great education isn't about the type of school—home, public, private. It has a lot more to do with the type of learning: Lecture Method versus Discussion Method. Therefore, to really understand the problem with multiple-choice testing, we need to clearly realize that this is a serious challenge for all parents: no matter what kind of schools our kids attend. All schools—public, private, home, higher education—need to address the dilemma caused by nationalized, standardized, multiple-choice exams.

A Test for All

In fact, here's a powerful standardized test we might offer all parents in our modern world:

> "How well do you carry out the great responsibility to always know the right individualized educational goals and objectives for each of your children—each week, every week? And, knowing them, how well do you implement them? Or, to what extent do you delegate— or simply leave—this vital parental duty to others?"

How do you score? How can you improve? Will you start today, right now?

What a great exam.

In other words, which is best: Napkins or place mats? It all depends on your goals. The key is to make sure that as a parent you really know and embrace the right goals for each child—every week. Nobody can do this as well as a loving, dedicated, focused parent.

Once you know this, and live it, selecting the right kind of testing will come naturally and easily.

The Huge Problem with Multiple-Choice Exams

Let's try another exam question of the same kind:

> Question: What is the problem with multiple-choice tests?
>
> Answer: Well, it depends…

Really. That's the best answer. Nearly always. "It depends…"

C.S. Lewis taught in *The Abolition of Man* that all schooling has a design, meaning that each curriculum and testing arrangement is designed to bring about certain results. And many great educational thinkers from all sides of the education debate have agreed with this idea—from Dewey to Montessori, and from Adler to Jacques Barzun, for example.

So, to get straight to the point, what are multiple-choice exams designed to do to (and for) students? To explore this question, let's use a little comparison.

Oral exams (including informal discussion) naturally focus on what the student has learned, and how effectively he or she *thinks*. Oral examiners ask a question, listen to the answer, and then respond with further follow-up questions. In Socratic form, they notice an area of hesitation in the student's response, a clear error, or a potential weakness. And so they follow up with additional questions to see if this is really a lack of knowledge and understanding, or if perhaps the student simply misspoke. (With today's technology, some elements of this are as easily and effectively done online as in person.)

Likewise, the examiners witness a strength, or even a talent, and ask the student to share more of it. In this way, oral exams can very effectively arrive at an overview and outline of what the student knows and doesn't know, cares about or doesn't, has prepared for or not. Most of all, this format allows the examiner to see if the student can think creatively and independently, and how well he can do both. Again, this works in formal oral examination and also in simple, informal discussion.

To a lesser extent (because it isn't as interactive), an essay exam can discover a great deal about what the student knows about a topic. I have frequently scheduled three-day exams for college students and asked essay questions like:

> "Write everything you know about the Federalist Papers. List all 85 and comment on each. Take your time. Be thorough."

> "List every year from 1770 to the present year, and write at least one major event (what happened, why it was important, how it influenced later events, etc.) for each."

The results often ran to forty or more handwritten pages of solid, excellent summary, annotation, commentary, and thinking. Some were much longer, in the hundreds of pages. Essay exams test knowledge where oral exams more effectively test a combination of knowledge, understanding, wisdom, and the ability to think.

Projects, reports, research papers, and other such assignments are other forms of examination, even though they are not always considered so in the United States. Depending on the specifics of the project, they test different things. In general, such individual or even group assignments test the ability to understand what is expected, plan and work to deliver it, and then implement the plan and follow through. This naturally tests one's initiative, innovation, work ethic, delivery, and tenacity. These are all vitally important skills.

Point #1

In short, the best education includes all of these modes of testing: oral exams, essay exams, projects, reports, and research papers—especially after age 15. Why not learn *all* these lessons? Why leave any out? In fact, we should include multiple-choice tests in this overall model.

At their best, multiple-choice exams are designed to assess precision, rote memorization, and the ability to dialectically narrow down options to a single correct response. These are essential skills.

Point #2

The *second* point is that while multiple-choice exams are a good part of a youth's overall educational experience, in modern education they are often overdone, at the expense of other types of testing and their important lessons. Why not use fewer multiple-choice exams and more of the others? Why not reach for a meaningful balance that increases learning and excellence?

The problem with this is that most schools are actually compelled to teach to the tests in order to qualify for funding or to comply with laws that govern them. Teaching to the tests puts *schooling* ahead of *learning*, and this literally makes about as much sense as putting the cart before the horse. It simply doesn't work very well. When the means become more important than the objectives, something is awry, and quality always suffers under such circumstances. Our schools deliver mediocrity and failure much more often than they would if their focus was *learning*—rather than schooling.

Schooling is supposed to support learning, and it absolutely can. But on the issue of testing, particularly standardized multiple-choice testing, schooling frequently harms learning. It harms teaching. It harms studying. It harms thinking. In fact, it harms both analytical and creative thinking. And it frequently shuts down innovation and initiative.

How? Well, ask yourself: if you were to propose a different answer to a bubble test, because none of the answers offered fits, would that be rewarded, or would you be seen as a trouble maker or a smart aleck? Or just score lower on the exam?

If you were to argue with each of the answers, demonstrating why they were weak, would that get you brownie points with your teacher or administrator? If your experience was anything like mine, the answer is **NO**.

Testing like this is designed to celebrate and reward conformity. No kidding: I remember being shut down when I was trying to think about the answers in non-traditional ways, and told, *for the love of Pete*, to try to just answer in the way that was expected. The student's job is to try to get into the mind of the test creator and provide the answer they want you to.

Does this sound like leadership training? How much initiative, innovation and tenacity does this foster in kids that thrive in such a system? And to think that most of those who do not thrive are labeled as failures.

None of this is good for education.

Point #3

Third, and this is my main point, while multiple-choice exams do teach effectively in some fields, as a national standardized system they are a very bad idea—because their design is actually based on a flawed logic that is unknown to most people and deeply hurts our society.

What do I mean? Well, in fields where the answers to questions are very much a matter of thinking, not rote memorization, multiple-choice exams pit the "expert" answer against the student's natural tendency to think, reason, and innovate. This may in fact separate the scores of students who have learned to please the experts (usually labeled "good" students) from those who don't care what the experts think (often called "bad" students), but it creates a dilemma for a third group: those who care, but disagree; those who are thinking on their own (e.g. the natural leaders).

In short, in many cases multiple-choice exams—whatever academic subject they test and however the student scores—leave the following lessons quietly but indelibly imprinted on many test-takers: **If you get the right answer, you're smart; if you get the wrong answer, you're not smart; the experts determine the answer; so your purpose isn't to think, it's to agree with the experts; smart people agree with the experts; your independent and creative thinking isn't smart.**

Are there logical leaps in this progression? Certainly. But the flawed lessons are there as well. And there is at least as much logic supporting any of these statements as rejecting them. How can a young mind not wonder: "Why else would the adults put so much value and weight on these tests? Obviously, agreeing with the experts is the path to success and happiness in life."

Let's consider this same point from another angle, using different words and examples. Imagine you take the following test, in a highly emotional, competitive schooling environment where you are repeatedly told by those in authority that such tests will determine your success, status, progress, earning levels, and to a large extent your happiness in life. In this emotionally charged state, you sit and try to answer the following:

How many truly excellent ways are there to test students?

    A. One
    B. Two
    C. Three
    D. More than Three
    E. None of the Above
    F. All of the Above

G. It Depends

Which is the best way to test students?

A. Multiple-Choice Questions
B. Essay Questions
C. Assignments/Projects/Reports
D. Oral Questions
E. None of the Above
F. All of the Above
G. Two of the Above
H. It Depends

Of course, these exact questions aren't really on any test that I know about. [Thankfully.] But they are implicit in every multiple-choice test any student ever takes. Think about this for a moment. This is huge!

The saddest part of this is that the most correct answer, "It Depends", doesn't actually show up on most exams. It is implied, but the experts, the authorities, don't allow it. It doesn't fit their agenda.

The Hidden Code

This form of testing is a good example of many actual exams in which, ironically, the only possible correct answer differs according to an unwritten code. This is a serious problem. How is one to know when the "code" is in play, and when it isn't? What, in fact, is the code? Why is there an unwritten code in the first place?

To address these concerns, let's back up to the first time a child takes a multiple-choice exam. A number of things are going on when this happens. For example, the child probably has no idea there is a "code." Nor does the child have any idea what the code actually is. Nor has the child ever pondered that the code is designed to reward those who conform to the views of the experts and simultaneously "put in their place" those who think in other ways. So, as a result, the child takes the exam, guided by nothing except his or her innate senses and any instructions given by an adult.

For some children, this turns out to be a victory. Their good memory helps, but ultimately it is their innate sense of pleasing authority that helps them mark the answers they've heard from the adults in their life. They are quickly labeled the "good" students. (Assuming, of course, that the parent or teacher uses an exam designed "of the experts, by the experts, and for the experts"—as most modern multiple-choice exams are.)

But for other children this seminal event is much less promising. Let's say, for example, that the student's innate senses are much more attuned to reasoning things out in his own mind, or taking in the evidence from her personal experiences and applying them to each question on the exam, or even doodling on the side of the exam because he innately feels happier and learns more when he activates what popular psychology would call his "right brain creativity."

Such students will very likely get poor marks on the test. As a result, parent-teacher conferences will be held, adults will worry about and plan for these children, and the kids may even sense from a whisper, a glance, or a word that something has changed in how the adults now think of them. They might even receive a stern lecture from Dad or Mom.

Of course, the opposite will occur if the teacher or parent chooses, or by simple accident uses an exam designed to test the child's reasoning ability—not his attunement to the "right" answers so highly valued by the experts. In such a situation, many in the first group will feel the sense of loss while many in the latter groups will be told they are smart. An entirely different result will occur if the test is designed to find a student's creativity. But how is each student supposed to know "the code" in every exam?

Certainly the reality is much more complex than this little example. But over time, test after test after test, grade after grade, many a child learns to either run with his initial tendencies or find ways to suppress them. He is, inevitably, taught to accept the "expert" approach to learning if he wants to succeed in most schools.

And whether he comes from Group One or Group Two, he learns that "good," "smart," "gold star" students take multiple-choice tests the "expert" way, by turning off their thinking, creative, independent, innovative brains and focusing on the rote, accepted, repetitive, expert way of arriving at answers. Not every test is necessarily part of this system, but most are.

The Fallout

The great tragedy is that this choice bleeds into other aspects of the young person's life. How could it not? If tests are so important—and all the adults are emphatically asserting that this is inarguably the case—then certainly the world is made in the image of such tests. Right?

The pathway to success is obvious in such a world: rote, repetitive, risk-averse, non-creative, dependent but safe, trusting without really challenging assumptions; and, most importantly, truly applying yourself, working very hard to excel, and doing these things better than anyone else does them! Get the rote, safe, accepted answer more frequently than your peers. In fact, get it every time. Get it without fail. Always pass the test.

Never fail. Failure is…*dun-dun-dun*:

FAILURE!

Don't learn from failure; just don't fail. Don't risk; just become better at what the experts want. The lesson is clear: This is the path to good grades, scholarships, acceptance, success, advancement, promotion. Even in programs that promote multi-lane thinking, like law schools, such thinking is still frequently expected to conform to clearly delineated norms established by teams of experts.

The fact that such paths usually lead to what has been called "high-class drone work" or "highly-paid repetitive careers" isn't the point. Or, more accurately: it's the whole point! The goal. The objective. The plan. The definition of a successful life.

When multiple-choice tests are seen as the most significant, seminal, indicative measurement of a student's success, the student learns that failure is to be avoided at all costs, that his own self-worth depends on his ability to regurgitate information, and that a life filled with more of the same (high-class drone work and never thinking outside the box) is normal and right. This kind of life, where a person's main goal becomes "getting a good job no matter what," frequently robs the passion from life. It often leads a person to feeling like he/she is trapped in a job that isn't fulfilling, "succeeding" in earning an income but failing miserably at living a mission-filled life. Our children deserve better.

Accuracy and Reality

Let's take a step back from the modern addiction to nationalized tests and get real. The difficulty is that the answer to most exam questions should be "It Depends." Every time. On every multiple-choice test.

That's a bold statement. But just consider:

1. How many truly excellent ways are there to test students?

    A. One
    B. Two
    C. Three
    D. It Depends

2. Which is the best way to test students?

    A. Multiple-Choice Questions
    B. Essay Questions
    C. Assignments/Projects/Reports
    D. Oral Questions
    E. None of the Above
    F. All of the Above
    G. It Depends

3. Solve the problem: $1 + 1 =$ _____. Mark the correct answer:

    A. 2
    B. 3
    C. 5
    D. 1
    E. X
    F. All of the Above
    G. None of the Above
    H. It Depends

Now, to repeat, here's the kicker: The best answer to all three of these exam questions is "It Depends."

Why? Not for the reasons you might think. First of all, "it depends" is the best answer because it is the most interesting answer. In fact, it's the only interesting answer of those provided. And that's the point: When the answer has to be one of those provided by the experts, the creative and independent part of the student's thinking automatically shuts down—at least a little. And frequently a lot.

Yet the best answers, the *great* answers, any groundbreaking or truly innovative answers, will always come when no solution is provided and you have to use your initiative, innovation, and thinking to come up with something excellent.

Think about it. The student who sincerely answers these questions with "It Depends" is thinking.

In other words, in giving the answer "It Depends" to a question like $1 + 1 = $ _____, the respondent is telling us something amazing about himself. He is "out of the box." He can see other alternatives. Most people trained in the multiple-choice era simply don't see any alternatives. They have been taught to not even *look* for alternatives. With such training, it never even occurs to them that alternatives might exist. In other words, they aren't thinking. Or even *trying* to think, for that matter.

The student who honestly answers "It Depends" isn't dependent on someone's list of options. He can innovate. He isn't bound by the so-called "right" answer provided by the experts. In all the years of training and schooling and being told the "right" answers and the "right ways" to find the right answers, and even to "show his work" to prove how he got the right answers in the "approved" way, he has kept a bit of himself apart from the conveyor belt, aloof from pleasing the experts, and independent of doing things just to fit in.

Moreover, by not just marking "2" he is saying that he does *not*, in fact, care about impressing whoever is administering the test more than about thinking, pondering, considering, and looking beneath the surface. To the world "of experts, by experts, and for experts," he may be seen as a rebel.

Good. Where thinking and innovating are concerned, we need more rebels. By definition, if you are doing things the accepted, normal way—the way sanctioned and outlined by the experts—you aren't actually innovating. We need more who think outside the box. More leaders, more trailblazers, more inventors, more artists, more who deeply challenge assumptions and seek for better ways—our world hungers for these.

Schools and Tests that *Cause* Decline

Our current societal decline is, at least in part, a result of our sad deficiency of originality, initiative, innovation, and truly independent thinking. And multiple-choice tests are designed to decrease such traits even more broadly in the general population. They naturally train "excellent sheep", as William Deresiewicz wrote about in his challenging book by that title. Allan Bloom referred to this very trend as "the closing of the American mind." Emerson attacked the way too many schools focus on conformity of thinking rather than educating self-reliant, thinking young people. Steve Jobs spoke of our great modern scarcity of dreamers and innovators.

The educational battle has in most circles become a competition to win the contest of The Top Rote Learner, The Best Expert Pleaser, and The Superior Moderately-Paid Drone Careerist. And multiple-choice tests are essential to this model. They aren't its only feature, to be sure, but without them this system would dwindle. They are part of its glue, its ether, its essence.

They may, in fact, *be* its essence. What would our conveyor-belt schooling/career system be without standardized, nationalized, multiple-choice exams? Literally: nothing. It would collapse.

And what hardly anyone will admit, if they even realize it, is that the rote-nationalized-multiple-choice-and-lecture approach actually makes it more difficult to master the 9 Skills. People who spend a lot of time in this system find the 9 Skills more challenging—the Skills feel alien, even. This is a tragedy.

The one-size-fits-all system of schooling always under-delivers genuine *learning* and creates a funnel to credentialist elitism at the top. We are becoming an aristocracy because the gap between the super-rich and the rest keeps growing—and it starts with this type of education. Elites train their youth to be thinkers and risk-takers, using great books and the Discussion Method of learning.

Non-elites typically focus on the Lecture Method of schooling and multiple-choice exams. Such exams are designed by the experts to sort the populace, and keep the best and the brightest in the middle class—working for elites, but not competing with them.

That's not the answer. The ideal is something much better—a truly educated populace, where all are independent, creative, deep learners and thinkers. Adults as well as students.

Too idealistic? Maybe. But this goal is worth fighting for. And the solution to the current "rote-conveyor-belt/drone-work-careers/excellent-sheep-bureaucratic" model is true educational diversity: Let every family ponder, study, consider and choose wisely the best educational path for each individual child and youth—depending on various different, and constantly changing, personal student needs. Let the market respond accordingly.

Freedom actually works. We should give it a chance in the field of learning. To the extent that we do, *learning* will overtake schooling—to the huge benefit of all society, of the whole populace, not just a few dominant elites.

The Second Reason!

But, before we go on, there's one more thing. There is a second reason that the most accurate solution to $1 + 1 =$ _____ is "it depends." What is it? Well, in fact, "it depends" is actually the most accurate.

What does this mean? For most people trained on the conveyor belt system of modern education, the rote method has trained them to think that $1 + 1$ is 2. And it can be, under certain circumstances. But what the large majority of people educated in this era of rote factory-style learning were never taught is that $1 + 1 = 2$ has never been proven. Why? Because no mathematician has ever been able to prove that $1 = 1$.

In fact, $1 = 1$ is an unproven axiom, meaning that mathematicians just accept it even though they can't prove it. There is a long history of great mathematicians and scientists who tried to prove that $1 = 1$, and that therefore 1 + 1 = 2, but the best they could come up with is to start their mathematics with the postulate:

Let 1 = 1

Then they built everything else, including 1 + 1 = 2, on top of this foundational assumption. But the foundation is still unproven. In fact, it has been widely disproven. For example, if you are talking about apples, 1 *never* equals 1. There are no 2 apples that are truly the same. Add the element of time, and the same apple is different than itself after a moment of time has elapsed.

The only way any 2 apples are identical is numerically, meaning in our metaphysical mathematical minds or what Plato called "The Ideal." Not in physical reality. As Steven Covey argued, 2 + 2 should equal 5 or more as often as possible. This is called synergy. 2 + 2 = 4 is a very limiting belief. And it is based on dogma, not evidence. Not fact. Not reality. Again, 1 never equals 1 in the physical universe. Only in our minds. Only theoretically.

So, yes, if you are only working a math problem, then 1 + 1 might equal 2 because humans long ago decided to "Let 1 = 1." But there are many times in the real world where 1 doesn't equal 1. In fact, the *only* place 1 = 1 is in theoretical mathematics. So, if the question is posed as it was above ("Solve the problem: 1 + 1 = _____"), the truly most accurate answer, mathematically and otherwise, is either "X" or "it depends." Note that X in this equation means variable, or just another way of saying "it depends." If you are using theoretical math and you have defined your terms based on "Let 1 = 1", the answer is 2. If you are not, the answer is "it depends."

But since the question above didn't specify, then it depends. Period.

In short, the student who marked "it depends" got it right while all those who marked "2" technically got it wrong. The ones who chose "2" weren't just trying to please the experts; most of them actually don't understand the mathematics. Thus the sheep aren't all that excellent after all. And that's a huge problem in our educational system, because many multiple-choice questions on our nationalized exams (in all subjects) are like this.

Thinking vs. Rote

The elite classes have traditionally taught their offspring how to think; the masses too often teach their children what to think (and the "what" is determined by experts who are funded by elites). This is an effective model for maintaining a class system with a few elites running things from the top, but it's not good for democracy and it's a direct attack on free enterprise and opportunity for everyone.

This was Allan Bloom's biggest concern when he wrote *The Closing of the American Mind*. John Taylor Gatto, former New York state public school Teacher of the Year, wrote about the same problem, and he titled his book by the apt name *Dumbing Us Down*. Indeed, our dumbed-down education model has created a perpetual class system—exactly what the American Framers worked so hard to overcome. The crux of this modern American class system, at least at the educational level, is nationalized multiple-choice testing.

Again, we need more than one kind of testing to get it right, because not every student is the same—any more than your 1 apple is the same as any other 1 apple. And while the number 1 can be used numerically in theoretical mathematics, when we are talking about a human teen's life potential and goals, we need something much more accurate, more relevant, more informative. We need to help each one of them get a superb education, and that means one size doesn't fit everyone.

Let there be many kinds of schooling, and many kinds of tests. Some will prove beneficial to great learning, while others will not. And over time those most effective will flourish and grow. But all will be available to the individual student who needs one or two of them to really flourish.

This kind of educational buffet only thrives in a free system. Let there be as many kinds of tests as there are children with different educational needs, goals, talents and dreams. Yes, this makes *schooling* more challenging, but it is great for *learning*. And it is necessary to maintain a truly free society.

Let the variety of tests grow so there is a truly excellent testing model to match each student. And, most importantly, let there be many discussions about math, and every other field of learning. Not just "right answer" in a multiple-choice test. But real discussion, so each student understands everything we've discussed here—and more.

That's great education. Nothing else comes close.

Is this kind of Discussion-Based, truly personalized education and testing for every single student even possible at a national level? Perhaps. Perhaps not. But it is certainly possible in most homes and families. Starting with yours.

When the fundamentals of education fall short, as they do in the Lecture-Based model where youth are graded and sorted based on how well they measure up to the hidden expert-designed code (all for the continuing benefit of the elite class), rather than learning to truly think, initiate, create, innovate, and lead, we have a serious problem. That's the conveyor belt.

The Discussion-Based model of great books and great ideas is the solution. Note that this is precisely why through history the elite classes have delivered this very kind of learning (in what is almost exactly what we call Scholar Phase) to their own children.

Postscript: The Cards 2.0

What about students who want to excel in the multiple-choice exam system? Sure, it might not be the best model for every student, and it is a bad overall system for the nation because it is designed to drive a further wedge between elites and their middle- and lower-class "underlings." But if Johnny wants to be a doctor or an accountant, he's going to need to find a way to succeed in the system—however good or bad it may be.

To thrive on multiple-choice exams, become very good at using The Cards (as discussed in the last chapter). And use them to prepare for exams. This is incredibly effective. It really works. To do this, review the details in the previous chapter and apply the system to test prep.

10
Virgil's Prophetic Message for Today's Parents and Youth

"Teach me, thy tempted subject…"
−SHAKESPEARE

"Being in love with learning is a real passion,
a temptation to the right things, a fire of fun and learning."
−HANDWRITTEN NOTES ON TWO GENTLEMEN OF VERONA

"Do, or do not. There is no try."
−YODA

THE great Roman thinker Virgil has a lot to teach us. Most people don't read Virgil these days, or think about his suggestions, and that's a shame.

Virgil had a great deal to say that is directly relevant to our current world, societal, and family challenges. He lived at a time when Rome was the most powerful nation in the world, but he understood from the trends, cycles, and current events that the great superpower of his era was in serious decline—even though most people in "the Establishment" didn't want to admit it.

So he wrote about how his powerful nation could reverse its decline and get back on track. Win back its freedoms and virtues. Be the kind of example everyone in the world would want to follow. Reboot its morals, families, and educational system while spreading prosperity and true principles.

Sound familiar? We live in the same kind of situation right now in modern America.

Of course, Rome didn't listen much. But Virgil's writings remain. The American founders saw them as a timely commentary on the coming decline of the British Empire, and they acted accordingly. In our day, his messages are incredibly relevant. Let me share just one example.

Four Kinds of Education

As I said, Virgil watched Rome losing many of its freedoms, and he saw how the educational system had a direct impact on this decline and loss. In Virgil's view, education should be based on the interactions of four kinds of learning: the epic, the dialectic, the dramatic and the lyric. I forget where I first read about these four types of education in a commentary on Virgil, but knowing how these all fit into our modern world is both interesting and important.

1. *Epic Education* means learning from the greatest stories of humanity in all fields of human history and endeavor, from the arts and sciences to government and history, from math to technology, and from leadership and entrepreneurship to family and relationships. Epic education is education from the great classics—and other works of similar quality.

   By seeing how the great men and women of humanity chose, struggled, succeeded, and sometimes failed, we gain a superb epic education. We learn what really matters. The epics include all the greats—from the great books of world religions to the great classics of philosophy, history, literature, mathematics, art, music, etc. Epic education focuses on the great classic works of mankind from all cultures and in all fields of learning.

2. *Dialectic Education* uses the dialogues of mankind, the greatest and most important conversations, discussions, and debates of history and modern times. This includes biographies, original writings and documents that have made the greatest difference in the world. It is also very practical and includes on-the-job style learning. Again, this tradition of learning pulls from all cultures and all fields of knowledge. It emphasizes mentoring.

Dialectic learning especially focuses on areas where debating sides and conflicting opponents came to resolution and taught humanity more than any one side could have without opposition—from wars and negotiations to debating scientists, to arguing preachers and the work of artists, inventors, etc. Most of the professions (medicine, consulting, finance, law, accounting, engineering, etc.) use the Dialectical learning method—also known as the Discussion Method of learning.

3. *Dramatic Education* is that which we watch. This includes anything we visually experience in dramatic form, from theater to cinema and movies to television and YouTube videos, reality TV programs, online tutorials, gaming, etc. In our day, this has many venues, unlike the two or three dramatic forms of learning available in Virgil's time. There is a great deal to learn from Dramatic Education in its many classic, modern and current modalities.

4. *Lyric Education* is that which is accompanied by music, or sound, which has a significant impact on the depth and quality of how we learn. It was originally named for the *lyre*, a musical instrument that was usually accompanied by a song during a play, poetic or prose reading. Some educational systems still use classical (especially Baroque) and other types of music to increase student learning of languages, memorized facts and even science and math. And, of course, most Dramatic (media and entertainment) learning is presented with music. Lyric Education also includes audio learning, anything we listen to. Note that the Lecture Method of most modern schools is based on the Lyric model.

The Current Battle for Education and for Our Future

With Virgil's outline of these 4 kinds of education as our background, let's remember that the future of education is very much in debate today. My reasons for addressing this here are:

1. Too few people are engaged in the current discussion (The Great Conversation) that will determine the future of education.

2.   Even most who *are* part of the discussion are focused on things like public vs. private schools, brick-and-mortar vs. online and/or home learning, funding, testing, minimum literacy standards, teacher training, regulations, credentials, policy, etc.

Specifically, digital technology has changed everything regarding education, meaning that in the Internet Age the cultural impact of the Dramatic and Lyric styles of learning over the other types threaten to undo American education and the strength of families, freedom, and prosperity. In short, success and freedom in any society depend on the education of the citizens, and when the Epic and Dialectic styles of learning disappear, freedom soon declines.

And make no mistake: The Epic and Dialectic (classics, discussion, mentoring) models of learning are everywhere under attack. They are attacked by the political Left as elitist and unavailable to most people, and they are attacked by the political Right as unnecessary for one's training in a career specialty.

They are attacked by techies as old, outdated and at best quaint. They are attacked by the professions as "worthless general ed courses," and by too many educational institutions and governments as "useless to getting a job." But most of all, and this is far and away their most lethal enemy, they are attacked by the simple popularity and glitz of the Dramatic and Lyric (visual and audio, entertainment and interactive media).

I am not suggesting that the Dramatic, Lyric and other parts of the entertainment industry have an agenda to hurt education or freedom—far from it. They bask in a free economy that buys their products and glorifies their actors, singers, producers, directors, and other artists.

Nor are Dramatic and Lyric products void of educational content or even true quality and excellence. Many popular movies, television programs, musical hits, and online sites deliver fabulous educational value. Songs and movies, in fact, teach some of the most important lessons in our society and many teach them with refinement, quality and depth.

But with all the good such Dramatic and Lyric styles of learning bring to society, the reality is that both free and enslaved societies in history have had Dramatic and Lyric learning. In contrast, no society where the populace was sparsely educated in the Epics has ever been free or widely prosperous. Period. No exceptions. Epic and Dialectical education naturally train people to excel in the 9 Skills.

In other words, we need a drastic shift from Lecture-Based (performance/Dramatic/Lyric/delivered by an expert and passively watched by everyone else) education to Discussion-Based Learning (participatory/Epic and Dialectical/engaged by all learners, not just a few experts). The former widens class divides and deepens mass dependence on elites, while the latter educates leaders in all of us.

In the most free nations of history (e.g. golden age Greece, the golden age of the Roman Republic, the height of Ancient Israel, the Saracens, the Swiss vales, the Anglo-Saxon and Frank golden eras, and the height of freedom and prosperity in the United States, among others), both the Epic and Dialectic (classics, mentoring, and discussion) styles of learning have been deep and widespread among the regular citizens of the nation.

If we want to remain a free and prosperous society, we will resurrect the use of Epic and Dialectic education in our nation. And parents are most able, and likely, to do this.

If the parents don't do it, at least some of them, it won't get done.

Remember the vital skills of success for the 21st century global economy that we discussed in Chapter 1? Such skills include the following:

- Creativity

- Ingenuity

- Initiative

- Quality Analysis

- "How to Make a Difference in the World Without Going Broke"[15]

- "How to Find Great Mentors and Teachers, Connect With Powerful and Influential People, and Build a World-Class Network"

---

15   Items in quotations on this list come from Michael Ellsberg, 2011, *The Education of Millionaires.*

- "What Every Successful Person Needs to Know About Marketing, and How to Teach Yourself"

- "What Every Successful Person Needs to Know About Sales, and How to Teach Yourself"

- "How to Invest for Success" (Entrepreneurship)

- "Build the Brand of You" (More than just Resumes!)

- "The Entrepreneurial Mind-set versus the Employee Mind-set"

- Grit

- Innovativeness

- Independent Thinking

- Originality

- Financial Wisdom[16]

- Effective Risk-Taking

- Tenacity

These kinds of skills are naturally mentored in the Dialectic model of learning, but they seldom appear in Dramatic or Lyric style Lectures-and-Academic-Testing models. In short, today's 1960s-style schools are failing to give our students what they need.

Let's be clear. As the influence of the Internet and social media spreads and becomes increasingly ubiquitous and mobile, it is going to continue to drastically change education. The Dramatic and Lyric (audio-visual, interactive online, virtual/gaming/e-teaching) are going to grow no matter what else does or doesn't happen in education. This development could be good or bad, depending on what else occurs.

What remains to be seen is whether or not classics (Epic) and mentors/discussion (Dialectic) will be relegated to the dustbin of history or resurge to the forefront in the emerging educational systems of the future.

---

16   See Chris Brady, 2014, *Financial Fitness for Teens.*

The Consequences

If classics, mentors and the Discussion Method aren't a central part of 21st Century education, at least three things will happen:

The money/power gap between a small, rich, elite class and the rest of the people will continue to grow.

North America's middle-class lifestyle will follow European trends (more families will live in apartments, not houses; few families will own their own cars; nearly everyone will live in large cities; families will choose to have fewer children and become much smaller; taxes will increase considerably; etc.).

The size and intrusion of government will grow, socialistic programs will spread, the private sector will drastically shrink, and incomes will decline (except for that of the elites).

This is what has happened in every society that moved from a *balance* between all 4 kinds of Virgil's education to *dominance* of the Dramatic and Lyric over the Epic and Dialectic. When the Roman Republic declined into the Roman Empire, and then weakened even more, they called the new dominance of the dramatic and lyric by the term "Bread and Circuses".[17]

Today, we must make the choice to resurrect truly quality education. If we make the right choice, we will see education, families, prosperity, and freedom flourish. If not, we will witness the decline of these things. Indeed, we simply must make the right decision.

We must also realize that this is not a choice for the experts. If the educational or political Establishment makes this decision, it will almost certainly go the direction of Europe as outlined above, and our families and economy will suffer and weaken.

---

17   *Panem et circenses*, as referenced in modern times in *The Hunger Games* capital city, "Panem".

Take Action

It is time for more citizens and parents to do the things that bring strong families, increased economic opportunities, renewed freedoms, and get our nations back on track. As Virgil put it long ago:

> Now the last age…
> Has come and gone, and the majestic roll
> Of circling centuries begins anew;
> Justice returns…
> With a new breed of men sent down from heaven…Assume
> thy greatness, for the time draws nigh

This is real. This is now.

And it all hinges on parents making the right educational choices for their families. In short, we must no longer settle for mediocre education and schooling; we must instead accept nothing less than truly great learning.

The key to this choice is Scholar Phase. The 9 Skills are vital. A generation or individual that gets Scholar Phase will naturally move toward leadership, success, and societal progress. Any generation — or youth — that doesn't, won't.

Carpe diem, as the ancients said. Seize the day.

The truth is that Virgil's "new breed of men sent down from heaven" wasn't really a new breed at all. The youth simply received quality Discussion-Based education (Dialectic) in the Great Books (Epic). This changed everything, but the process is simple and easily understood.

In our day, it is time to replace the old-style Industrial Age high school with something better, something more suited to the technological and economic realities of the 21st century. In other words, it is time to implement Scholar Phase. To bring down "a new breed of learning" that restructures our current declining model of elite-controlled conveyor-belt schooling for the masses. As Virgil put it: "Assume thy greatness, for the time draws nigh…" In other words, Hero Education.

This can be done in schools, in classrooms, in front of computer screens, at home, wherever parents, mentors and young people focus on great reading and Discussion-Based learning. But it must be done. Scholar Phase changes everything.

Indeed, Scholar Phase is the education of the future. Those who get a quality Scholar Phase will reap the leadership, economic, and societal benefits that have always gone to the brave souls who adapt to new realities and seize the day.

That day has arrived.